AFRIC CULTURE & AMERICAN BUSINESS IN AFRICA

HOW TO STRATEGICALLY MANAGE CULTURAL DIFFERENCES IN AFRICAN BUSINESS

Emmanuel Arthur Nnadozie

AFRIMAX, INC.
International Business Consultants & Publishers
Kirksville   Charlotte   London

African Culture & American Business in Africa
How To Strategically Manage Cultural Differences in African Business

By Emmanuel Arthur Nnadozie

Published by:

AFRIMAX, Inc.
P. O. Box 946
Kirksville, Missouri 63501

Publisher's Cataloging-in-Publication
(Provided by Quality Books, Inc)

Nnadozie, Emmanuel U
    African culture & American business in Africa : how to strategically manage cultural differences in African business / Emmanuel Arthur Nnadozie. — 1st ed.
    p. cm.
    Includes bibliographical references and index.
    Preassigned LCCN: 97-73858
    ISBN 0-9658867-4-3

    1. United States—Commerce—Africa. 2. Africa—Commerce—United States. 3. Business etiquette—Africa. 4. Corporate culture—Africa. 5.Africa—Social life and customs. 6. Business enterprises, Foreign—Africa. I. Title. II. Title: African culture and American business in Africa.

HF3132.N66 1998   338.8'8973'06
                                   QBI97-41015

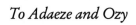
To Adaeze and Ozy

CONTENTS

List of Boxes, Tables, and Figures.. 7
Acknowledgments and definitions.. 8

INTRODUCTION   11

1 WHY DO BUSINESS WITH AFRICA?   15

Ten Major Reasons Why Americans Should Do Business With Africa, 15
A Note of Caution, 28
US-Africa Trade at a Glance, 29

2 CULTURE AND BUSINESS IN AFRICA   30

Culture Includes Patterns of Behavior, Values, and Attitudes, 31
African Cultures are Diverse and Complex, 32
African Culture Influences Business Behavior, 32
Differences Among National Cultures Follow Five Dimensions, 34

3 AFRICAN CULTURAL DIMENSIONS   37

Africa has High Social Inequality and Considerable
Dependence of Subordinates on Bosses, 38
Titles, Formality, and Prestige are Taken
Very Seriously in African Cultures, 40
Personal Relationships and Connections are
Key to Successful Business in Africa, 41
African Societies Tend to be Collectivist, 42
African Societies are Male-dominated, 44
In Dealing with Uncertainty, Africans Emphasize
Harmony More than Conflict , 46
Africans have a More Relaxed Attitude Toward Time than Americans, 48

Tradition and Honor are Highly Regarded, 50
Bribery and Corruption are on the Rise, 51
Rules and Regulations are not Always Obeyed, 52
Other Cultural Manifestations, 53
Summary of the Most Common Cultural Characteristics, 54

4 MANAGING CULTURAL DIFFERENCES IN AFRICAN BUSINESS — 55

Leading, Communicating, and Implementing, 56
Showing Respect for Formality, Hierarchy, Titles, and Age, 58
Establishing Personal Relationships and Connections, 60
Managing Masculinity and Femininity, 60
Dealing with Tradition and Honor, 61
Adapting to "African time" and the African Concept of Time, 61
Surviving the Corruption Dilemma, 63
Dealing with Indiscipline at the Business and Societal Levels, 65
Enhancing Work Ethic and Improving Worker Productivity, 65
Dealing With Nepotism, 67
The 3 Ps of African Business: Pensiveness, Patience, and Perseverance, 68
Improving Intercultural Communication, 68

5 UNDERSTANDING AFRICA — 73

Myths and Facts, 73
Africa is a Very Diverse Continent, 74
Anglophone, Francophone, and Lusophone African Cultures Differ, 76l
Religion and Business in Africa, 78

CONCLUSION — 82

Notes 84
Appendix 88
Index 105

BOXES

Box 1. Profile of Often Ignored Progress 26
Box 2. African Entrepreneurial Cultures 49
Box 3. An Example of Misunderstanding
    Across Cultures 64
Box 4. An Example of What Not To Do 71

FIGURES

Figure 1. Steps Involved in Managing Cultural
    Differences in Africa 56
Figure 2. The Diversity of Africa 74

TABLES

Table 1. Africa Compared With Other Regions.................................... 17
Table 2. Africa's Emerging Markets 20
Table 3. A Comparison of the American
    and African Business Cultures 33
Table 4. Indexes of Cultural Dimensions for West Africa,
    East Africa, South Africa, and the United States
    Obtained from Hofstede's Indexes 39
Table 5. Comparison of African and American Cultural Dimensions 54

ACKNOWLEDGMENTS AND DEFINITIONS

ACKNOWLEDGMENTS

Many individuals provided valuable comments and other kinds of support. Special thanks are due to Shawna O'Grady for her insights and assistance with the articulation of cultural differences. Particular thanks are due to Professors Bennie Nunnally, Chudi Uwazurike, Vicki Crawford, Seymour Patterson, Dorothy Ruiz, Lucinda C. Grey, and Bob Sherman. My heartfelt gratitude goes to Roberta Duff, Evas Dusabe, Tracey Lantz, Paula Presley, and Tim Rolands.

ACRONYMS AND ABBREVIATIONS

AfDB	African Development Bank
CFA franc	Currency known in West Africa as the *franc de la Communauté financière d'Afrique* (franc of the African financial community) and in Central Africa as the *franc de la Coopération financière en Afrique centrale* (franc of the Central African financial cooperation)
FAO	Food and Agricultural Organization of the United Nations
FDI	Foreign Direct Investment
FCS	Foreign Commercial Service
GATT	General Agreement on Tariff and Trade
GDP	Gross domestic product
GNP	Gross national product
GSP	United States Generalized System of Preferences

IFC	International Finance Corporation of the World Bank
IDV	Individualism Index
IMF	International Monetary Fund
LTO	Long Time Orientation
MAS	Masculinity Index
MIGA	Multilateral Investment Guarantee Agency
NGO	Nongovernmental organization
OPIC	Overseas Private Investment Corporation
PDI	Power Distance Index
SPA	Special Program of Assistance for Africa
STO	Short Time Orientation
UAI	Uncertainty Avoidance Index
UNDP	United Nations Development Program
USAID	United States Aid for International Development
USDIA	United States Direct Investment in Africa
USFDI	United States Foreign Direct Investment
WTO	World Trade Organization

Warning—Disclaimer

This book is designed to provide helpful information for people doing business with African countries or people wishing to understand the African business culture. It is sold with the understanding that neither the author nor the publisher is engaged in legal, medical, accounting, or other professional services. For such services please contact a competent professional.

Every effort has been made to provide complete and accurate information. However, there may be errors of omission or typographical mistakes. The text should, therefore, be used only as a guide and not as the ultimate authoritative source on information about African culture, cultural differences, international business, or American business with Africa.

If you do not wish to be bound by the above, you may return this book, in good condition, to the publisher for a full refund.

INTRODUCTION

From Tunis to Cape Town and from Dakar to Mogadishu, African societies exhibit unparalleled dynamism and changing attitudes. Several countries are currently linked to the information superhighway; some of them even have CNN or other European networks. This is a market ripe for picking by American business. But the American businessman and woman must understand that they must compete with Europeans who have several centuries of historical relationship with Africans as well as Asians, who currently are aggressively pursuing African markets.

The American entrepreneur also needs to see that a company's success or failure in Africa will depend on its ability to understand and adjust to Africa's dynamic market. He or she must educate himself or herself about African culture and approach African business with an open mind. This publication, through the author's personal observation and knowledge and through interviews and research, provides an analysis of cultural characteristics that define the African business culture and strategies for successfully managing cultural differences.

There are four important questions to ask about cultural differences to insure business success in Africa:

1. What specific characteristics define African business culture and does the latter differ from American business culture?

2. What are the implications of these cultural characteristics for American business?

3. What effective strategies can be used to successfully manage cultural differences in Africa?[1]

4. What factors shape the continent's culture?

Based partly on research developed by Geert Hofstede and others, these major cultural characteristics can be identified in Africa:

■ Africans have high social inequality and considerable dependence of subordinates on bosses.

■ Africans have a remarkable respect for hierarchies, titles, and age.

■ They tend to place a lot of importance on personal connections and relationships.

■ Africans are more collectivist than individualistic.

■ African societies are male-dominated

■ They consider time as flexible, not always firm, hence the so-called "African time."

■ They think tradition and honor are very important.

■ They may not adhere to rules and discipline because rules are not always enforced.

■ African workers have a positive work ethic, but tend to be relatively less productive.

The complex and changing African environment requires business men and women and managers to have a degree of flexibility and freedom in managing business with Africa to respond to subtle or major differences in various countries. The potential for turbulence also requires businessmen and women to constantly monitor and assess the political risks in the countries with whom they are doing business.

The explanation of the most common African values and business culture that I have provided in this book should improve ones sensitivity in relating to Africans. It is, however, important to note that business culture varies widely from nation to nation. The differences are influenced by values, historical, economic, and social realities of each country. Similarities do however, exist and that is what this book focuses on.

HOW THIS BOOK IS ARRANGED

The first chapter explores the main reasons why American businessmen and women should consider doing business with Africa. The first chapter also cautions against possible risks associated with African business. The second chapter gives a working definition of culture, shows the complexity and diversity of African culture, and indicates that African culture influences business behavior. This chapter gives the five dimensions of differences among national cultures and compares the American and African business cultures. The third chapter highlights major African cultural dimensions. This is done within the framework of social inequality, relationship between the individual and the group, concepts of masculinity and femininity, ways of dealing with uncertainty, and concepts of time. The fourth chapter suggests ways of effectively managing cultural differences in Africa by making specific how-to recommendations, including how to improve intercultural communication. Finally, the fifth chapter gives pertinent information necessary for the understanding of the African continent and the factors that shape its cultures.

1

WHY DO BUSINESS WITH AFRICA?

TEN MAJOR REASONS WHY AMERICANS SHOULD DO BUSINESSES WITH AFRICA

In 1995, America's foreign direct investment (FDI) went mostly to high-wage industrialized countries—with the United Kingdom topping the list—rather than to low-wage developing countries. The pattern of US foreign direct investment was driven by factors other than low wages. Even though there was a record 15 percent increase in US FDI in 1995, the share of the $711.6 billion of American FDI that went to Africa declined from 3 percent in 1982 to a mere 1 percent in the late 1980s, and held steady thereafter. At the same time that American direct investment to Africa was declining, the share of total American FDI to Asia and the Pacific increased from a mere 9 percent in 1982 to 22 percent of total in 1995.

Although American investment in Africa is on the decline, here are 10 major reasons why Americans should do business with Africa.

Africa is the most profitable market in the world!

African business is profitable and, indeed, more profitable than elsewhere, says the US Department of Commerce. According to the Commerce Department's reports, US investment in Africa—by American multinational firms in natural resources, manufacturing, and services—has also outperformed US investment worldwide. It "generated a 30 percent return on book value, compared with 11 percent worldwide, 14 percent in Latin America, and 12 percent in Asia and the Pacific region." [2]

The US Commerce Department also reports that "US direct investment in Sub-Saharan Africa by non-bank US affiliates generated net income of $1,092 million in 1994.[3] Thus the Commerce Department's reports not only indicate comparatively higher profitability, but they also show that "US direct investment in Africa consistently generates high rates of return." The Department's trade reports show that "during the period 1990-1994, the average annual return on book value of US direct investment in African was nearly 28 percent, compared with 8.5 percent for US direct investment worldwide." [4]

Despite this higher-than-average return on book value, American investment in Africa remains low, concentrating on the petroleum sector. This situation raises two main questions: Are American firms unaware of Africa's lucrative markets? Are they focusing on factors other than profits in deciding whether or not to do business with Africa?

With a population of nearly 700 million people, Africa represents a huge market that cannot be ignored

Africa represents a significant market that the US cannot afford to ignore. According to the US Department of Commerce, in 1991, Africa imported almost $99 billion worth of goods. That's hardly an amount to ignore. Sub-Saharan Africa imported $63.3 billion worth of merchandise in 1994 (down from $67.4 billion in 1980). The major imports are capital goods (mostly plants and equipment), intermediate consumption goods, and transport equipment.

Table 1. Africa Compared With Other Regions

	Area (million square miles) 1992	Population (millions) 1992	GNP (millions of US dollars) 1990	GNP per capita ($) 1990	Imports (thousands of US dollars) (c.i.f.)	Exports (f.o.b.)
Africa	11.6	656	398,840	640	98,645	90,582
South America	6.8	302	650,580	2,230	67,770	64,005
China	3.6	1,165	415,880	370	63,957	62,812
South Asia	1.9	1,187	374,670	330	38,948	37,586

In 1995, the countries of Sub-Saharan Africa represented a total import market of $81 billion, while their combined exports totaled nearly $76 billion. The buying power of Africa's 656 million people may not be as high as that of Americans or Europeans, but as rational consumers Africans need goods and services such as medicine, automobiles, computers, management training, education, factories, etc. There is, therefore, a market to be exploited.

In 1990, per capita income for Southern Africans was $2,260, more than six times that of the Chinese. Even the average West African earned more than the average Chinese (see Table 1). Why then is there a rush to invest in China and not in

Southern or West Africa?

African countries have embarked on substantive political
and economic reforms, and attitudes are changing all over the
continent

From the Cape to Cairo, African countries have embarked
on historic political and economic reforms; they have also made
remarkable improvements to create business-friendly markets.
Thus, in addition to political reform there has been improvement in accountability, predictability, and rule of law. Notably,
over 25 countries have held democratic elections since 1990. In
terms of economic reform, more than 30 African countries
undertook the IMF and World Bank economic stabilization and
structural adjustment programs involving currency devaluation,
privatization, price and trade deregulation, removal of subsidies, budgetary controls, etc.

The following countries (with a population of 500,000 or
more) were considered by the World Bank to have reasonable
social stability and adjustment programs in place during 1987-
1991: Benin, Burkina Faso, Burundi, Cameroon, the Central
African Republic, Chad, Congo, Côte d'Ivoire, Gabon, The
Gambia, Ghana, Guinea, Guinea-Bissau, Kenya, Madagascar,
Malawi, Mali, Mauritania, Mozambique, Niger, Nigeria,
Rwanda, Senegal, Sierra Leone, Tanzania, Togo, Uganda, Zambia, and Zimbabwe.

Attitudes and policies are changing rapidly in Africa. The
economic restructuring and trade liberalization embarked upon
by many African countries are indicative of this change in
attitude. There is "a growing recognition that, given the proper
support, the enterprising energies of Africa's people have enor-
mous potential," write Keith Marsden and Thérèse Bélot in a

World Bank publication.[5] Likewise, there is growing recognition that deregulation as well as cooperation and collaboration with foreign enterprises has generated positive results for African enterprises.

According to a report submitted by the President of the United States to the United States Congress:

> ... *change has begun to sweep the African continent as countries are increasingly abandoning the discredited statist policies of the last three decades and committing to policy changes based upon democratic political principles and market-based economic reforms. This growing commitment to democracy and structural adjustment inspires optimism about the future of Africa and provides new opportunities for the United States both to support African efforts and to pursue American economic and security interests.*[6]

It is equally noteworthy that in an attempt to increase the size of the fragmented markets regional blocs are emerging. The Economic Community of West African States (ECOWAS) and the Southern African Development Community (SADC) are two examples. The existence of a common currency, the franc CFA, among many francophone African countries makes business easy across these countries.

Africa is the ultimate emerging market

With 14 countries having stock markets and 5 more in the process of establishing markets, Africa is well under way to developing competitive capital markets. Calvert New Africa Fund, which is blazing the trail in the development of African stock market, thinks and believes that "With its vast natural resource base, extensive labor supply and unique geographic location, Africa represents the ultimate emerging market." This American investment company gives five reasons why Africa should be the ultimate choice of investors: 1) Africa trades more with the US than the former Soviet Union and Eastern bloc countries combined. 2) Aggressive reforms have taken place in more than half of all African countries. 3) Nigeria and Angola are major oil exporters to the United States. 4) The accounting standards used in Africa's emerging markets are based on internationally acceptable norms. 5) Africa will benefit enormously from increases in prices of the critical commodities it supplies the world.[7]

Table 2. Africa's Emerging Markets

Country	Capitalization in billions of US dollars	Country	Capitalization in billions of US dollars
Egypt	2.5	Mauritius	0,4
Morocco	1.9	Botswana	0.3
Nigeria	1.2	Côte d'Ivoire	0.3
Kenya	0.6	Ghana	0.08
Zimbabwe	0.6	Tunisia	0.05

South Africa has the largest Stock Market in Africa with more than 650 companies and a combined market capitalization exceeding $240 billion (Calvert New Africa Fund Web Page).

Africa is now represented among the world's emerging equity markets according to the International Financial Corporation's (IFC's) *Emerging Markets* Data Base (EMDB), the premier source for comprehensive statistics on stock markets in developing countries. Ten African countries are featured among IFC's list of emerging stock markets.

Dr. Seymour Patterson, Professor of Economics who spent a Fulbright year in Botswana, had this to say:

> *It is important to address the notion that a catastrophe in a country in Africa is tantamount to catastrophe in all of Africa. In Africa, there are a lot of places where things are beginning to work at some level, maybe not at the European or American level, but the opportunities are there. Some countries are fairly stable and opportunities abound for businesses to take advantage of cheap labor. If you look at the profile of each country, most of them have done well over the decade, especially before they became straddled with overwhelming debt. Therefore, a strong case can be made for strong foreign investment in Africa.*[8]

Major American companies are already in Africa; some have been there for over 30 years

Many American and European companies, including such transnationals as Coca Cola, Exxon, Texaco, Chevron, and IBM have been operating profitable business in Africa, some of them for over three decades. If these companies consider Africa a viable market, why do not other entrepreneurs? "At year-end 1994, the U.S. direct investment position in Sub-Saharan Africa was" according to the US Department of Commerce, "$3,672 million. $1,044 million of the position was in South Africa, $567 million in Angola, and $402 million in Nigeria."[9] South Africa and Nigeria represent about 62 percent of US trade with Sub-Saharan Africa. Six other African countries—Angola, Côte d'Ivoire, Ghana, Ethiopia, Kenya, and Zimbabwe—account for an additional 19 percent of US exports to Africa, according to the President's report to the US Congress.

It is, therefore, important to note that major multinational companies do business in Africa in spite of the continent's negative press. Small businesses, especially African American businesses, need to get on board to take advantage of the reformed economies, cheap labor, limitless opportunities, and substantial profits.

The US Government has increased support for American firms engaged in African business

The US Government—especially the Clinton administration through the late Commerce Secretary Ron Brown—has established strong and unprecedented initiatives and created resources and technical support to encourage American business in Africa. These initiatives include the various trade missions conducted by the Commerce Department and congressional action. In September 1996, Congressmen Phil Crane, Charles Rangel, and Jim McDermott introduced the trade and investment initiative bill for Sub-Saharan Africa. More specifically, "The bill," according to a statement issued by Congressman Jim McDermott, "establishes expanded trade and investment ties as an objective of U.S. policy and outlines several specific measures to achieve this goal, focusing on countries committed to economic and political reform, market incentives, and private sector growth. The bill sought to accomplish six things:

1. Establish a $200 million equity and infrastructure fund in 1998.

2. Establish a US-Africa Economic forum to facilitate annual high level discussions.

3. Develop a US-Sub-Saharan Africa free trade area by 2020.

4. Undertake Export-Import Bank initiatives.

5. Provisional removal of the safeguard provisions of World Trade Organization's Textile and Clothing Agreement for sub-Saharan African countries.

The Report of the President to the US Congress states:

> *The primary objective of the Administration's Comprehensive Trade and Development Policy is to work with the people and leaders of Africa in the pursuit of increased trade and investment, and sustainable economic development. Achievement of these objectives would, in turn, enable the countries of Africa to become more fully integrated into the global economy and share in the prosperity enjoyed by participating countries.*

This report specifies that the US government pledged to "focus its support on those countries in Africa that are pursuing meaningful structural adjustment and economic reform because they have the greatest chance of success," by:

- joining in multilateral efforts to assist those African countries undertaking meaningful economic and regulatory reform, including debt reduction where warranted;

- supporting efforts to improve essential government and non-government institutions;

- supporting efforts to improve physical infrastructure needed in a modern market economy;

- creating a more growth-oriented business climate that will attract foreign as well as domestic investment and generate expanded trade in which U.S. firms can participate as effective commercial partners;

■ removing barriers to trade in Africa and increase African participation in the world trading system, including the World Trade Organization, the U.S. GSP (Generalized System of Preferences) program, and strengthen intellectual property protection;

■ expanding advocacy and support programs for U.S. exporters and investors in Africa; and

■ promoting greater regional integration within Africa in order to reduce the problem of small-sized markets.[10]

American governmental and non-governmental organizations (NGOs) are now more supportive than ever

The private sector has also embarked upon a series of substantive initiatives to increase foreign business in Africa: NGOs and not-for-profit organizations such as Rev. Leon Sullivan's biannual African-African American Summit, Constituency for Africa, African-American Chamber of Commerce, Corporate Council on Africa, etc.

Such US government agencies as United States Aid for International Development (USAID) and Overseas Private Investment Corporation (OPIC) have played a key role in either assisting African countries in developing an enabling environment or in promoting trade and investment. The African Development Bank (AfDB) financed projects create an opportunity for American businesses to increase their business in Africa. Usually, the Foreign Commercial Service (FCS) in Abidjan, Côte d'Ivoire and the US Executive Director's Office at the Bank encourage US interest in the AfDB and will actively support US companies pursuing Bank business.

International organizations provide rules and safeguards against business risk

International organizations and agencies have established safeguards and rules of operation to encourage foreign businesses and protect investments. This is exemplified by the regulatory and supervisory role of the Multilateral Investment Guarantee Agency (MIGA), an affiliate of the World Bank Group, established in 1988 to promote the flow of private foreign investment to developing member countries; the World Trade Organization (WTO); the International Court at the Hague, etc.

In 1994, more than 120 countries, including African countries completed negotiation of the Uruguay round of the General Agreement on Tariffs and Trade (GATT). Under this agreement, six basic provisions were to be implemented: reduction of global tariffs, removal of trade–inhibiting rules, reduction of agricultural subsidies, new protections for intellectual property, phasing out of quotas on textiles and clothing, and the establishment of the World Trade Organization (WTO) to oversee the provisions of the agreement and to resolve any trade disputes under the new rules.

It is time to end the European domination and monopoly of the African market

With all the expansion occurring in East Asia, and with Europe and Japan becoming competitively difficult markets, it is hard to believe that Africa will not be the market of the future. It will be in any entrepreneur's strategic interest to enter this market now to increase his or her future competitive advantage. Nearly 60 percent of Sub-Sub-Saharan African imports come from Europe; only about 9 percent originate in the United States. The picture is pretty much the same for US imports from Sub-Saharan Africa.

> *African business will be beneficial to Americans and Africans*

Africa needs trade and investment, not aid and assistance. African countries need foreign investment to supplement domestic investment, strengthen their private sectors, engender technology transfer and spur economic development. Many African firms are waiting to form partnerships with American firms, especially in Comoros, Ghana, Gabon, Nigeria, Sey-

---

Box 1
Profile of Often Ignored Progress

Judging from African countries' colonial experience, remarkable progress has been made and there are, indeed, success stories. These indicators of economic development bear testimony to this fact:

Income: During 1960-1993 real per capita income increased for the majority of Africans

Education: Net increase in primary school enrollment by nearly two-thirds between 1960-1991

Health & Nutrition: Remarkable increase in life expectancies by over 33% between 1960 and 1993. Dramatic reduction in infant mortality rates. Remarkable doubling of the population with access to safe water. Four-fold increase in per capita food production in the past decade, despite rapid population growth.

Poverty: Some non-negligible achievement in reducing poverty.

Environment: Insignificant contribution to global emission by the continent.

Individual freedom: Democratic elections held notably in over 25 countries since 1990. Strong tendency toward political and economic reforms. Major achievement of the liberation of South Africa from its apartheid past.

---

chelles, South Africa, Zimbabwe, and Botswana. Americans will ultimately benefit from doing business with Africa because jobs will be created in America and incomes will increase.

Increased business with Africa will engender economic growth in Africa, and this would not only stabilize the region financially and politically, but also create greater opportunities for US businesses and investors and more jobs for Americans. Likewise, economic development in Africa will mean expanded trade with the United States, resulting in economic growth and new jobs for Americans as well as for Africans.

Africa is at the same time a place of incredible opportunities with considerable profits and a place with often difficult and challenging business opportunities. Unfortunately, business with Africa has not always been beneficial to the continent since historically the approach to African business has been to exploit, it not to invest heavily in it. For this reason, major infrastructure, support services and education were either ignored or geared toward facilitating this exploitation.

It is important also to know that political instability is not limited to Africa and cannot be an excuse for lack of foreign investment especially since it does not seem to matter elsewhere. Likewise, despotism is not the sole preserve of Africans as history has shown all over the world. African instability should no longer be a deterrent to major international business because several parts of Africa are more stable than other parts of the world in which considerable foreign capital has been flowing during the past decade. Actually, it could be argued that foreign investment reinforces stability since it generates economic growth and obligates the industrialized countries to protect their interests.

A NOTE OF CAUTION

Although Africa is the ultimate emerging market, it presents some risks and a certain level of uncertainty (see appendix for a list of types of restrictions, controls, and threats that may be encountered by foreign operations of American firms. Despite a record level United States foreign direct investment (USFDI) in 1995, the fact that over thirty African countries have reformed their economies, and the existence of highly lucrative and profitable business opportunities in Africa, the amount of US direct investment in Africa (USDIA) remains low and has, indeed, been declining since 1982.

Many African countries have stressed the need to expand private foreign investment, following structural adjustment and economic reform programs. However, the amount of USDIA has remained low and even declined since 1982. In Africa, relatively little is known about the reasons why the level of USDIA remains low and the best strategies to use to increase USDIA.

The picture in the African countries themselves is not always bright, thereby increasing business risk. Africa continues to experience serious economic difficulties despite economic reform—stabilization and adjustment—as evidenced by the lack luster performance of the majority of Sub-Saharan African countries in the post-adjustment period. Per capita GNP for the Sub-Saharan African was only $460 in 1994, showing a discouraging average annual growth of -1.2 percent during the period 1985-1994. The average annual growth rate of GDP for low-income economies excluding China and India was 5.8 percent in 1980-1990 and 6.2 percent in 1990-1994; for Africa, the GDP growth rate was only 1.7 percent and 0.9 percent respectively during the same periods.[11]

In a number of African countries there is a move toward the market system without a dynamic and vibrant private sector and in the face of numerous constraints. In almost all African countries, long-term growth prospects are being retarded by the lack of investment. Thus, even though there are investment opportunities, there is inadequate access to finance, particularly risk capital. This underlies the urgent need to encourage foreign direct investment and "...accelerate the development of local capital markets in developing countries."[12] Capital is a critical issue in enterprise and private sector growth.

The decline in public investment and diminishing foreign investment has serious implications, especially in light of the threat they pose to the long-term growth prospects of African countries. For instance, of the 37 African countries shown in the *World Development Report 1996*, 26 registered declines in the net private capital flows between 1980 and 1994, only 9 countries showed increases, while 2 remained unchanged.[13]

US-AFRICA TRADE AT A GLANCE

- US-Africa trade increased in 1966. US exports to Sub-Saharan Africa was $6.1 billion in 1996;

- The growth in US trade with Sub-Saharan Africa was higher than the growth in US-global trade;

- Nigeria and South Africa continue to dominate US-Africa trade;

- US is Africa's leading market;

- US exports to SSA increased 14 percent over 1995;

- SSA accounts for less than 1 percent of total US exports;

- Crude oil accounts for a disproportionate 70 percent of US imports from Sub-Saharan Africa;

- US-Africa trade is dominated by primary products imports by the US, especially minerals.

The future of American business with Africa is bright, provided the efforts made by the public and private sectors to provide information and support are maintained. There are two sides to the issue of increased American business with Africa. The first is related to economic growth and political stability in African countries and the second is related to the action of the US government. For Africa to become a major attractive market, African governments must establish sound economic policy and ensure transparency and accountability under a democratic and business-friendly environment. Likewise, the US governments must intensify its effort to provide information, support, and guarantees to American businesses in order to encourage them to do business with Africa.

2

CULTURE AND BUSINESS
IN AFRICA

CULTURE INCLUDES PATTERNS OF
BEHAVIOR, VALUES, AND ATTITUDES

Culture is "...a frame of reference consisting of learned patterns of behavior, values, assumptions, and meaning which are shared to varying degrees of interest, importance, and awareness with members of a group." "...It cannot actually be seen or touched," but we can generally recognize these learned patterns when we notice them. Elements of culture include how people relate to each other in a society, the structure of the society, and social organization. "In studying culture, we are studying the common rules, the common assumptions, the common values that are the foundations of the external behavior which we can see, touch, and feel."[14]

AFRICAN CULTURES ARE DIVERSE AND COMPLEX

African culture is diverse and very complex. Indeed, we cannot talk of one African culture but of African cultures. For convenience we talk of African culture in terms of a representative sample of the different African cultures or as the ensemble of common manifestations from different parts of Africa

African culture has always been dynamic and responsive to internal and external pressures. Recent developments in world history are bound to affect its dynamics. We can categorize African culture into traditional, modern, and contemporary. Traditional African culture involves the way of life before Europeans came to Africa. Modern African culture is the way of life since the colonial period. Contemporary African culture is the African way of life today, marked by the end of the cold war and by the information age.

Furthermore, African culture has been made more complex by the appearance of Islamic culture in the continent. In some cases the Islamic culture eliminated the existing traditional culture; in others they synthesized into a hybrid. Colonialism is another important external influence on African culture. Africa has not remained static, as many anthropologists would make us believe. African culture has imbibed what it needed from outside while retaining its authenticity.

AFRICAN CULTURE INFLUENCES
BUSINESS BEHAVIOR

Based on the definitions given earlier, we can state that culture is also the sum total of human knowledge and acquired behavior of humankind. Societies have a set of behavioral rules that are transmitted from one generation to another. How these sets of rules operate, impinge upon, and apply in the business setting is the business culture of any society.

Culture determines values; values shape attitudes; attitudes influence business behavior. That's why it is important to understand how African business culture differs from American business culture (see Table 3) and how African culture can affect American business in Africa. But the diversity and complexity of the African social groups make it difficult for us to generalize about common cultural characteristics. Because of regional, ethnic, religious and cultural diversity, there are bound to be differences within African countries. We can, however, minimize this problem by assembling cultural manifestations and differences into distinctive groupings or dimensions, based on how societies deal with basic problems. To do this, we have to rely heavily on characterizations developed by experts.

Table 3. A Comparison of the American and African Business Cultures

United States	Africa
High degree of competition and independence among businesses leading to head-to-head competition among companies	Competition is not a dominant principle; communalism and group dynamics are the dominant principles
Discouragement of government controls and influence over the private sector by use of laws and regulations designed to preserve competition	Great deal of government control and straddling that sometimes de-emphasizes, even discourages, competition
Perception of competition as good and healthy; cooperation within industries or between government and industry as wrong, unhealthy, and suspicious	Harmony and cooperation means working for the benefit of the whole, not necessarily based on a long-term vision
Belief that lack of competition will create lack of motivation to innovate and reduce overall productivity	The entire establishment and all management practices are aimed at eliminating competition for the most part

DIFFERENCES AMONG NATIONAL CULTURES FOLLOW FIVE DIMENSIONS

In his book, *Cultures and Organizations: Software of the Mind,* Geert Hofstede, a Dutch social scientist, refers to a "mental programming" that appears in different layers, corresponding to different levels of culture. These layers include the national, regional or ethnic, gender, generational, social class, and corporate levels. "In modern societies," Hofstede argues, these cultural layers "...are often partly conflicting: for example, religious values may conflict with generational values; gender values with organizational practices." Furthermore, Hofstede states that "Conflicting mental programs within people make it difficult to anticipate their behavior in a new situation."[15]

Findings of Hofstede and others show that national cultures differ in five dimensions:

- The degree of integration of individuals within groups

- Differences in the social roles of women versus men

- Ways of dealing with inequality

- The degree of tolerance for the unknown

- The trade-off between long-term and short-term gratification of needs

These five dimensions originate from Alex Inkeles and Daniel Levison's suggestion that the following issues qualify as common basic problems worldwide: relation to authority; perception of self, in particular, the relationship between individual and society, and the individual's concept of masculinity and femininity; and ways of dealing with conflicts, including the control of aggression and the expression of feelings. Inkeles and Levison also believe that these problems have consequences for the functioning of societies, of groups within those societies, and of individuals within those groups.[16]

Based on these differences identified by Inkeles and Levison, Hofstede developed the following criteria and used them to study IBM employees in various countries:

1) Social inequality, including the relationship with authority

2) The relationship between the individual and the group

3) Concepts of masculinity and femininity: the social implications of having been born as a boy or a girl

4) Ways of dealing with uncertainty, relating to the control of aggression and the expression of emotions.

Thus, Hofstede developed a four-dimensional (4-D) model of establishing cultural differences among countries: Power distance (from small to large); collectivism versus individualism; femininity versus masculinity; and uncertainty avoidance (from weak to strong). A fifth dimension established by Hofstede and Michael Bond is time orientation, or more appropriately Long Time Orientation (LTO). LTO values are persistence, order and thrift, while Short Time Orientation (STO) is the opposite pole indicating steadiness and stability, respect for tradition, saving face, and reciprocation of favors and gifts. In this publication, the classification and discussion of common cultural characteristics of the African business environment follows the dimensions identified by Hofstede and adds other dimensions as well.

3

AFRICAN CULTURAL DIMENSIONS

To understand the cultural aspects of doing business in Africa, the following five specific questions relating to African business culture are important to answer:

1. How do people in Africa deal with social inequality, including the relationship with authority? For instance, how do they view hierarchy, titles, age, etc. and what role does personal relationships play in their interactions?

2. How does the individual relate to the group in the business or societal arenas? Do people tend to be individualistic or do they tend to be communal or collectivist?

3. What are their concepts of masculinity and feminin-

ity? That is, how does people's perception of assertiveness versus modesty play out in business?

4. How do people deal with uncertainty, relating to control of aggression and the expression of emotions? Do Africans cherish harmony over conflict?

5. What is the people's attitude toward time (long-term orientation versus short-term orientation), honor, rules and discipline, ethical issues, and the work ethic?

AFRICA HAS HIGH SOCIAL INEQUALITY AND CONSIDERABLE DEPENDENCE OF SUBORDINATES ON BOSSES

What is the significance of position and how does it relate to hierarchy, titles, age, etc.?

The position of an individual is mostly dependent on his or her age and social status.

POWER DISTANCE

Power distance is defined as "the extent to which the less powerful members of institutions and organizations within a country expect and accept that power is distributed unequally."[17] Institutions are the basic elements of society such as family, school, and the community. Organizations are places where people work.

To measure the degree of inequality in the society, Hofstede used the Power Distance Index (PDI), which ranges from small power distance to large power distance. Based on his survey of IBM employees in 50 countries and 3 regions, he recorded large power distance values for Latin countries (including France and Spain), Asian, and African countries. He also recorded low values for the USA and Great Britain.

The large PDI for African countries (see Table 4) is consistent with the existence of considerable dependence of subordinates on bosses. This is characterized by centralization of power. Because subordinates expect to be told what to do, supervision is essential. Also, businesses have more structure and hierarchy, with superiors getting privileges. Hofstede suggests that "...Packaged leadership methods invented in the USA, like management by objectives (MBO), will not work [in high power distance societies] because they presuppose some form of negotiation between subordinates and superiors which neither party will feel comfortable with."[18]

Table 4. Indexes of Cultural Dimensions for West Africa, East Africa, South Africa, and the United States Obtained from Hofstede's Indexes.

Index	West Africa	East Africa	South Africa	United States
PDI	77	64	49	40
IDV	20	27	65	91
MAS	46	41	63	62
UAI	54	52	49	46

West Africa (Ghana, Nigeria, and Sierra Leone); East Africa (Ethiopia, Kenya, Tanzania, and Zambia). PDI = Power Distance Index; IDV = Individualism Index; MAS = Masculinity Index; and UAI = Uncertainty Avoidance Index.
Source: Figures used in the table were obtained from Hofstede's data.

TITLES, FORMALITY, AND PRESTIGE ARE TAKEN VERY SERIOUSLY IN AFRICAN CULTURES

Africans have a remarkable respect for hierarchies, titles, and age.

Greeting is very important in all of Africa. Before talking about business, one must inquire about health and family. In African countries, people want to be properly greeted and properly addressed as Chief, Doctor, Engineer, Barrister, etc. People are also expected to show a great deal of politeness and courteousness.

The importance placed on titles, formality, and prestige is underscored by the respect for hierarchy, titles, and age. With the exception of a few African countries such as South Africa, where reasonable migrations have taken place in the recent past, the continent is made up of indigenous people. As a member of the group, the individual's social worth is often based on age. Age determines status in the society. Age or status are the most important determinant of respect and leadership. Behaving correctly is important for the individual as a member of the group.

Among the Yorubas of southwestern Nigeria, respect for age is very important. In this case, one must address an older individual as "Sir." It is not unusual to see younger people genuflecting or prostrating themselves when they are greeting an older person. If an individual is perceived as lacking respect, he will experience a lot of difficulties.

For example, a special guest at a Nigerian wedding ceremony refused to take his place at the "high table" and, indeed, forbade his wife from doing the same because the master of ceremony addressed him as Mister instead of Chief Reverend Doctor.

Examples of titles that people want to be identified with are the following: Professional titles such as Barrister Umaru, Engineer Okoro, Honorable Chief Owusu, Doctor Bode, as well as the positions in the organizations including President, Managing Director, Chief Executive, Monsieur le Directeur, President Directeur Generale (PDG), and so forth.

One must understand the hierarchy that exists within the organization to avoid starting off on the wrong foot. The organizational setup is in most cases rigid, and centralization ensures that not many people can make decisions. One must therefore ensure that they are negotiating with the right person, the person who can make decisions.

Thus, employees work more for their boss than for the company. It is not uncommon to actually notice some reluctance even among professionals to challenge authority. Because submission is mostly rewarded rather than independent thinking, it is important to understand this reality and not mistake it for lack of innovation or personal motivation.

PERSONAL RELATIONSHIPS AND CONNECTIONS ARE KEY TO SUCCESSFUL BUSINESS IN AFRICA

What role does personal relationship and "connection" play in doing successful business in Africa?

Africans tend to place a lot of importance on personal connections and relationships.

Americans and Africans have different views on the role of

personal relationship in business. In Africa, there is need for personal trust and for establishing a trusting relationship. A great importance is attached to the family and the extended family. Thus the notion of family may be more extensive than that in the United States—there is often the use of brother or sister among people who are unrelated.

It may be difficult to speak to an executive without going through an intermediary. The African will need to know you personally to establish some kind of trust. This will require a reasonable amount of time and effort directed toward cultivating relationships, sometimes in informal and familial settings. In francophone Africa, it is widely believed that one could never get anything done—including obtaining a license or birth certificate—unless one know somebody or goes through somebody who knows somebody.

Despite the explosion in communication that marks the information age, most African businessmen and women one may encounter are used to doing first time serious business face-to-face and not through the fax or the telephone.

AFRICAN SOCIETIES TEND TO BE COLLECTIVIST

In addition to emphasizing personal connection, Africans are more collectivist than individualistic.

INDIVIDUALISM VERSUS COLLECTIVISM

Individualism refers to a cultural situation "...in which the ties between individuals are loose: everyone is expected to look after himself or herself and his or her own immediate family." Collectivism occurs in "...societies in which people from birth onwards are integrated into strong cohesive ingroups, which throughout people's lifetime continue to protect them in exchange for unquestioning loyalty.[19]

Although degrees of individualism and collectivism vary within and among countries, it is clear that African countries are more collectivist—unlike the United States which is more individualistic. Again Hofstede's study confirms this through the Individualism Index (IDV) values, which was high for the United States, low for East and West Africa.

Unlike the United States, African countries tend to be collectivist societies. Thus in the majority of African countries, the interest of the group—family, village, town, ethnic group— prevails over the interest of the individual. This collectivism is manifested in several ways but mainly through the existence of the extended family structures. In this case people mostly think in terms of "we" instead of "I." This collectivist culture is clearly expressed in the popular African saying: "It takes a village to raise a child."

Individuals do not easily give their opinions freely. Resources are shared and dependency is high and sometimes problematic for the income earners in the extended family system. Every individual is expected to take care of his or her kin—parents, direct brothers and sisters, uncles, cousins (including distant ones), and even "relatives" one does not know that one has. Individuals owe ritual and financial obligations to the family.

A friend complained bitterly about the difficult and painful experience he had when his mother visited him in the United States after nearly 10 years. According to him, they could not agree on anything and there was tension. He had developed the American direct-talk direct-response attitude, which did not please his mother, to whom the less direct attitude is preferable. She expected the family to maintain control over his son's affairs and demanded his undivided loyalty. When these became impossible, she complained that her son no longer owed allegiance to the family and accused him of abandoning his heritage.

In business, collectivism has many advantages. It can foster group dynamics and team effort, which is known to have enabled the Japanese to successfully develop highly competitive industries. This is because collectivism associated with harmony and cooperation means working for the benefit of the whole, based on a long-term vision, rather than the benefit of constantly changing individuals.

Getting into high positions is largely affected by family connection as opposed to education or merit. This means that harmony is preferred, and relationship is important. This also means that nepotism is a common feature in both public and private sectors. People will generally (and they are expected to) hire people from their immediate family, town, or ethnic group whenever there is an opening. This is what the Igbos call *ima mmadu* (the ability to know people or connection) and in Yoruba we speak of *kporakpoism*.

AFRICAN SOCIETIES ARE MALE-DOMINATED

How do Africans' perception of masculinity and femininity, assertiveness versus modesty, play out in the work place?

Even though Africans tend to be modest and focused on quality of life, being born male gives the individual more opportunities than being born female.

MASCULINITY AND FEMININITY

"Masculinity pertains to societies in which social gender roles are clearly distinct (i.e., men are supposed to be assertive, tough, and focused on material success; whereas women are supposed to be more modest, tender, and concerned with the quality of life)." On the other hand, femininity "... pertains to societies in which social gender roles overlap (i.e., both men and women are supposed to be modest, tender, and concerned with the quality of life)."[20] While women find working conditions, work hours, and method of supervision to be important, men find earnings and opportunity for advancement to be important. While men desire to supervise others, women tend to emphasize the relationship with the supervisor.

Hofstede uses the Masculinity Index (MAS) to measure cultural differences among nations and regions. This index is based on 0 for most feminine and 100 for most masculine. In Hofstede's study, Japan (95) was most masculine while Sweden (5) was most feminine. Hofstede also found out that Anglo countries tended to be moderately masculine and South Africa (63) fits this mode. However, with a respective MAS of 46 and 41 the West and East African countries studied by Hofstede were surprisingly on the feminine side, whereas the United States (62) was moderately masculine.

The analysis of masculinity and femininity according to occupation fits well with the situation found all over Africa where men dominate the ranks of better-paying jobs: they are salesmen, professional workers (engineers/scientists), skilled workers/technicians; while women constitute the majority of unskilled and semiskilled and office workers. Recall that women's role in African societies became further complicated by both Islam which limited their rights—in some cases considerably—and Westernization and Christianity (including Western education) which gave rise to functional marginalization. This marginalization occurs when women are disproportionately represented in the clerical and secretarial positions with no real opportunity for upward mobility.

Although the African countries represented in Hofstede's study are moderately feminine, like many other societies, African societies are male-dominated. Thus, being born male gives the individual more opportunities than being born female. In African societies women are respected but because of their subordinate position in the society, they tend to aggregate at the lower rungs of the workplace.

Another important characteristic found in Africa is modesty. Modesty is a virtue highly cherished all over Africa; however, assertiveness is not uncommon among some cultures and this can play out in the workplace as well.

IN DEALING WITH UNCERTAINTY, AFRICANS EMPHASIZE HARMONY MORE THAN CONFLICT

Do Africans emphasize harmony more than conflict in dealing with uncertainty or in the expression of their emotions?

Africans prefer harmony to conflict.

AVOIDANCE OF UNCERTAINTY

Uncertainty avoidance is "...the extent to which the members of a culture feel threatened by uncertain or unknown situations." According to Hofstede this feeling is, among other things, expressed through nervous stress and in a need for predictability: a need for written and unwritten rules.[21]

Hofstede measured avoidance of uncertainty by means of the Uncertainty Avoidance Index (UAI), scoring 0 for a country with the weakest uncertainty avoidance and 100 or above for the strongest. His findings show that African countries had medium to low UAI scores.

It is possible that because France scored a high (86) UAI, that francophone African countries, which are not represented in Hofstede's study, may have higher uncertainty avoidance than anglophone countries. Great Britain's UAI of 35 was also low as was the United States' UAI of 46.

Africans do not generally feel threatened by uncertain or unknown situations. In this case, "what is different" is not necessarily dangerous or ridiculous, but maybe curious. To avoid embarrassment or conflict, many Africans may prefer to make something up, since saving face and maintaining harmony is of utmost importance in these cultures. Africans try not to disappoint people; they try as much as possible to avoid conflict, and hence to be harmonious. In trying not to disappoint, Africans may say "yes" to avoid conflict since they are more oriented towards harmony than conflict. This behavior obviously may appear to Americans to be dishonest or to lack integrity.

AFRICANS HAVE A MORE RELAXED ATTITUDE TOWARD TIME THAN AMERICANS

Africans have a more relaxed attitude toward time and they view time as flexible.

THE QUESTION OF TIME

The phrase African Time—established time plus a few hours—would not have been invented if time perceptions did not differ between Africans and Americans. To many Africans, time is considered not firm but flexible. This is not an indication of a lack of seriousness but rather a totally different perception of time. Generally, people will be at work on time and students will attend lectures on time; but chances are that they will treat other time-based arrangements such as meetings, social activities as more flexible. Interestingly enough, this view of time is not unique to Africa. American businessmen and women are likely to encounter the same views of time in some European and Latin American countries as well.

Many Africans do not believe in making decisions quickly. Things can be put-off until tomorrow. Even deadlines are very flexible. Africans have a more relaxed attitude toward time, deadline, and details. There may seemingly be a lack of a sense of urgency. One must understand that this attitude toward time is not related to lack of ambition; rather it is explained by the reality that people face in the bureaucratic culture that has emerged in the continent.

Due to the uncertainty that surrounds them, a lot of people focus on the past and the present rather than the future. Many

Box 2

African Entrepreneurial Cultures

The work ethic and business culture of some African societies have led to the emergence of modern enterprises which have the potential for growth. Keith Marsden shows that contrary to common belief, the middle is not missing in Africa; indeed, there is widespread existence of strong and vibrant African enterprises that can be "the pioneers of development in Sub-Saharan Africa."[22]

African entrepreneurship has three models of emergence and development: the spontaneous, state-induced, and institution-induced modes. The spontaneous model—exemplified by the Igbo entrepreneurship—encompasses those that are driven mostly by factors endogenous to the society in which it is found. The second model emerges as a result of government support and straddling as we see in cases from Kenya. The third, similar to the second, owes its emergence to concerted effort of non-governmental forces as we see in the case of the Mouride of Touba in Senegal, where religious forces have galvanized members of the sect into formidable entrepreneurs.

Deborah Brautigam reveals the accumulation of considerable industrial capacity in Eastern Nigeria, generated mostly by indigenous enterprises.[23] Moreover, African enterprises have been responsive to fiscal policy and deregulation. There is also evidence to show that African private enterprises are resilient and have the prospects for expansion. In addition to being creative, flexible, and adaptable, they are efficiently run modern enterprises in both the formal and informal sectors and they have developed market networks.

In the case of the Nigerian Igbos, that the main origins of entrepreneurs are diverse and that apprenticeship plays an important role. Likewise from 1970s to the 1990s, the emergence of graduates and younger professionals without public sector experience established themselves as the new generation entrepreneurs in Nigeria.[24]

There is also, in the case of the Nigerian Igbos, evidence of business diversification, partnerships, conscious effort toward the adoption of foreign technology and orientation towards exports. Apart from their increasing level of efficiency and sophistication, Modern entrepreneurs make positive contribution to the economy by alleviating poverty and engendering growth.

people have experienced national, societal, and political instability and the resulting uncertainties. It is, therefore, often difficult to plan for the long-term because people work to live, and they are concerned more about the present than the future.

Break time depends on colonial experience and religion. In general, the francophone countries are on lunch break between 12:00 and 2:00 p.m. Some government offices in some countries open at 7:00 a.m. and close at 3:30 p.m. In predominantly Muslim countries or in the Muslim parts of some countries Fridays are not working days. Sometimes only half of the day is devoted to work on a Friday to enable the Muslims perform their worship.

TRADITION AND HONOR ARE HIGHLY REGARDED

Tradition and honor are of great importance in many African Societies.

Saving face or protecting face is of utmost importance in the African culture. People will go to great lengths to avoid losing face or bringing shame to themselves and their family. People will take great care to save face, hence they will not readily admit ignorance.

In virtually all African traditions, the issue of honor is very important and people will take care to avoid dishonoring themselves. This means that a business partner may persist with an unworkable situation or a difficult circumstance just to avoid either disappointing his or her foreign partner or dishonoring himself or herself.

At times some Africans may not believe that "no" means

"no." So they may persist with the belief that the "no" may be changed to "yes."

Because people try to avoid actions considered to be dishonorable or shameful, they often talk about "soiling one's father's name," "selling one's self-respect," "shaming the family," etc. This means that an individual will strive not to soil his father's name, sell his self-respect, or shame his family. The danger here is that failure is greatly abhorred since it may be considered dishonorable. This attitude leads people to become too cautious and less adventuresome.

BRIBERY AND CORRUPTION ARE ON THE RISE

Several accepted practices in many African societies may be considered questionable in the United States.

Bribery exists in Africa as in other parts of the world; however, it is on the increase. This is readily the most difficult problem related to business practices to deal with. Bribery is illegal in all African countries. There are, however, several business practices that border on outright corruption. These can range from making a payment to get papers processed to paying the customs officer a certain amount to clear goods. They can sometimes involve openly being required to adjust contract figures by, say, 10 percent to accommodate the kickback that goes to government officials. Thus, the line between personal bribes and acceptable gratuities is often blurred.

A firm may face difficulty if it refuses to make a payment to get papers processed or to pay the customs officer a certain amount to clear goods. Likewise, a contractor can lose business for refusing to adjust contract figures by say 10 percent to accommodate the kickback that goes to government officials.

RULES AND REGULATIONS ARE NOT ALWAYS OBEYED

Rules and discipline may not be adhered to, not because Africans have a greater propensity to break rules but because the rules are not always enforced.

Certain rules and laws are often overlooked in favor of meeting the needs or desires of specific individuals. Some individuals constantly operate as if they are above the law. These are usually the elite, including the military elite, business elite, and political elite. There may be widespread disregard for simple rules and regulations set by law—ranging from traffic lights violation to public solicitation, mainly because of the lack of enforcement.

AFRICANS HAVE POSITIVE WORK ETHIC AND MANY SOCIETIES ARE VERY ENTERPRISING

African workers have a positive work ethic, but they may be relatively less productive.

Africans have a positive work ethic and in almost all African cultures, hard work is cherished and dignity of labor extolled. But productivity levels are likely to be lower than ideal because of low expectations and lack of skill. Notwithstanding this low productivity, many African societies present a formidable culture of entrepreneurial dynamism. For instance, the Nigerian Igbos, the Kenyan Kikuyus, and the Senegalese Mourides are known for their remarkable entrepreneurial ability.

OTHER CULTURAL MANIFESTATIONS

■ People are sensitive about the pronunciation of their names. They do not want one to be patronizing or to clearly show prejudice, bias, or stereotypical beliefs. One should not be condescending.

■ Among the Wolof of Senegal and in some parts of Ghana and Nigeria, children are taught not to look adults in the eye, since this is considered an act of defiance or a total lack of respect. This means that eye contact, considered as a mark of trust or truthfulness in the West, may not occur when some Africans are talking to their superiors.

■ In many African countries, using the left hand to receive or give gifts is considered impolite, and therefore, unacceptable. This is because the left is often associated with negativism.

■ In most African cultures, greeting is very important, so it is not unusual to see the same greeting, such as welcome, repeated several times.

■ Handshaking is very common in Africa, but it could range from a simple handshake, to prolonged, and sometimes vigorous forms. It is not unusual to find younger people, women, or subordinates offering both hands as a mark of respect. In most cases, women are expected to accept a handshake, not offer one.

SUMMARY OF THE MOST COMMON CULTURAL CHARACTERISTICS

Titles, formality and prestige are taken very seriously in African cultures. Africans place a lot of importance on personal connections and relationships. Africans are more collectivist than individualist; hence the interest of the group prevails over the interest of the individual. Africans emphasize harmony more than conflict in dealing with uncertainty. Africans have a more relaxed attitude toward time, which is viewed as highly flexible. Although tradition and honor are of great importance in many African countries, bribery and corruption are becoming common place. African workers have a positive work ethic, but may be relatively less productive.

Table 5. Comparison of African and American Cultural Dimensions

Africa	America
High Power Distance	Low Power Distance
Collectivist	Individualistic
Moderately Feminine	Moderately Masculine
Moderate to Low Uncertainty Avoidance	Low Uncertainty Avoidance

4

MANAGING CULTURAL DIFFERENCES IN AFRICAN BUSINESS

Strategic management (both in the long and short run) evaluates the mission of the organization, its objectives, and possible actions given the organization's environment. Business managers must think strategically in dealing with cultural differences. American firms must, therefore, devise competitive strategies to survive in the highly competitive African marketplace. Management of cultural differences would involve designing policy that is targeted toward the components of the cultural dimensions. Since profit is the primary objective of firms, business leaders must target strategic aspects of the business environment such as the business culture, set strategies to deal with cultural differences, and systematically encourage employees to become globally competitive. Strategic management of cultural difference is, therefore, necessary in order to achieve the goal of profit maximization.

Strategic management will also enable American companies to improve their performance and achieve the goals of the firm. Finally it will help to generate the right kind of image and connections that are vital for survival in the increasingly competitive African markets.

LEADING, COMMUNICATING, AND IMPLEMENTING

The following schema shows the steps involved in managing cultural differences in Africa:

Figure 1. Steps Involved in Managing Cultural Differences in Africa

The first step involves the identification of business cultural differences, that is, the most common African cultural characteristics. The next step is the acceptance of differences which involves tolerance and open-mindedness. The last step involves the actual management of cultural differences and the improvement of intercultural communication.

To successfully manage cultural differences in Africa, leadership by top management is essential to the much-needed commitment. When an American firm decides effectively to manage cultural differences, it must make organization-wide efforts and long-term commitment, accompanied by investment in training. The strategy to manage cultural differences must involve the following components:

Leadership: Leadership requires top management to be foremost in the area of developing knowledge of and sensitivity toward host-country cultures. In addition to clearly directing personnel, leadership must show vigor in the communication of organizational values.

Communication: Communication is a two-way process involving feedback. Communicating across cultures is, indeed a difficult task and must be carefully understood. In order to communicate effectively, the parties must be connected, open, and able to afford unbroken passage of information. Yet, intercultural communication is much more complex and more complicated. One must understand how to effectively communicate within an intercultural setting to become a winner. The issue of intercultural communication is further dealt with at the end of this section.

Implementation: Implementation involves the specific programs or cultural sensitivity training and activities geared toward minimizing culture shocks, uncertainty, prejudice and negative stereotyping. Indeed, the key element of implementation is the action taken to improve or to learn intercultural communication. To improve intercultural communication, Larry Samovar and Richard Porter recommend that an America must know himself or herself, consider the physical and human settings, seek to understand diverse message systems, develop empathy, encourage feedback, develop communication flexibility, and avoid stereotyping and prejudice.[25] These are the factors that can help improve intercultural communication.

SHOWING RESPECT FOR FORMALITY, HIERARCHY, TITLES, AND AGE

A good understanding of the hierarchy that exists within the organization helps one to avoid starting off on the wrong foot. Likewise, an understanding that the organizational setup is, in most cases, rigid and that centralization ensures that not many people can make decisions is equally important.

It is advisable to greet or address people by referring to their titles. It is not unusual to find Nigerians and some other Africans being referred to as Chief, Doctor, Sir, at the same time. Thus, the formality of title is very important in much of Africa. In addition to knowing the significance of the titles, care must be taken to address a potential business partner or counterpart in the way he or she considers appropriate to prevent being considered insolent.

The greeting ritual is also very important. An American on a business trip in an African country went to the post office to buy stamps. He noticed that the lady at the counter practically ignored him. When he succeeded in getting her attention, she proceeded with the transaction in the slowest and most unfriendly manner possible. The American could not help but notice that the lady did not appear to be happy with him. When he complained to other people about his experience, they advised him to show some courtesy the next time around. It dawned on him that all he needed to do was to say "Hi, how are you today?" to get not only a change of attitude from the lady but also very quick and friendly service. If one takes the time to perform the ritual of greeting or the preamble that precedes transactions, one will get better service. This is because business activity is not seen as a mere transaction.

One must also thoroughly understand the process of negotiation which for Arab Africans is a very important process. Not recognizing formality and traditions can affect business negotiation negatively. Other factors that can affect business negotiations are the cultural conditioning resulting from language, religious beliefs, ethical systems, and modes of interpersonal behavior.

One must, therefore, observe business protocol—in terms of appointment seeking, greeting behavior, formality—and the use of time in business negotiation. In this regard, it will be wise to note the importance of letters sent in advance, usually written in English, French, Portuguese, or Arabic. Often a go-between (an intermediary) will be necessary.

One must observe the greeting protocol of host country as much as possible. Because people tend to be formal and have different views of time, the American business person must exercise a great deal of patience and tact because the intended results may not come easily or quickly. Many Africans engage in lengthy greeting which should not be seen as abnormal or unusual.

Since the British emphasize the formality of doing business it should not be surprising that many former African British colonies inherited this tradition. In reality, the line between business formality and excessive bureaucracy is very thin, and this is where an American can get very frustrated.

ESTABLISHING PERSONAL RELATION-SHIPS AND CONNECTIONS

Any American who is new to African business must strive not to rush into anything. It is important to take time to understand a potential partner or business counterpart to ensure that both parties clearly understand what the partnership or relationship really means and what each party will do. The American businessperson must learn to build trust in a society that moves more slowly and makes decisions less quickly. One must also understand that in predominantly Muslim countries, adherence to strict Islamic rules means the avoidance of pork and alcoholic beverages. Disregard of this fundamental belief could jeopardize a personal relationship or connection.

Most Africans would want to get to know their business counterparts through conversations on a wide variety of issues. It is not advisable to try to conclude a major business deal or to try to engage in significant financial transactions without being there in person or being represented by a company executive or consultant. Success in securing a major business deal in many African countries often depends more on whom one knows than on what one can do. This makes it important to establish strategic relationships which are vital for success.

MANAGING MASCULINITY AND FEMININITY

The most important thing to understand here is that African countries are changing and evolving toward providing more opportunities for women. Indeed some countries have seen fit to establish ministries or departments of women's affairs. Unfortunately, the pace is still very slow in many countries.

Countries with a large Muslim population are really lagging behind in giving women more opportunity in the society. Companies must be ready to tap into the female human resource base of their host countries and in most cases should be prepared to take the lead in affirmatively providing women with the opportunity to rise up to leadership positions.

DEALING WITH TRADITION AND HONOR

Businesses can use the characteristic of honor to their advantage, provided they understand what is really involved in the avoidance of losing face or bringing shame to oneself and to one's family. Expectations must be clearly established and explained. Each employee or associate must be made aware of these expectations. Managers must clearly communicate that it is okay not to know everything, and that employees should be free to seek help or clarification. Employees must be made aware that it is not okay to say "yes" in order not to disappoint or to avoid conflict. They must be made to understand that continuing with faulty or wrong options in an attempt to avoid losing face will be costly to the company and will, therefore, be unacceptable. So one must be able to read the nuances and understand when "no" really means "no" and how to communicate exactly what one means.

ADAPTING TO "AFRICAN TIME" AND THE AFRICAN CONCEPT OF TIME

Care must be taken when scheduling a meeting to avoid break times, prayer times, Muslim and Christian holidays, etc. It is important to understand that if a business counterpart does not arrive in time it is generally accepted and should not be made much of. Other issues that require strict attention are the working hours, prayer time (especially for Muslims) and major holidays. A good knowledge of these time-related issues prevents making a major trip at the wrong time. For example, care must be taken to avoid scheduling a lunch meeting with a practicing Muslim during Ramadan (the Muslim fasting period).

There is no need trying to be in a hurry because often a great number of meetings and even several trips are required before a deal is sealed. Notably, once there is an initial success and trust is established, the future rewards can be considerable. Success will often come if an American businessperson ensures that the other party follows up on what it promised it will do. In other words, **follow-up is absolutely important and should never be taken for granted.**

This is because the African business counterpart may not see the need to be in a hurry about a business deal or because he operates within a bureaucratic culture that does not understand the need to be in a hurry in most cases. Also, if the business involves government offices or even financial or other institutions, these are often potential sources of unusual delays to the business transaction process. So follow-up is very important as well as an understanding that deadlines are flexible.

Because of the difficulties and uncertainties that people in various African societies have experienced, it is important to understand their point of view with respect to making long-term plans. Hence, people tend to focus on the present rather than on the future. This means that in order to get support for a forward-looking agenda, one must make sure that issues related to present situations or present gratification or to the security of workers or associates are not ignored.

SURVIVING THE CORRUPTION DILEMMA

The US Department of Commerce provides information and advice on how to deal with corruption and how to avoid dubious business offers in various countries. For help in determining what to do in the case of corrupt business practices or the legitimacy of a business proposal contact Office of Africa, US Department of Commerce, Washington DC 20230, fax (202) 482-5198.

The questions to ask in relation to bribery and corruption are: What should an American company do when competing for business with other international companies that may be willing to offer bribes? Is the benefit of getting a business worth the probable cost of breaking US and international law? Should an American company look for creative ways of avoiding direct involvement in corruption.

These are no easy questions to answer. The problem with bribes and kickbacks is that they can be very expensive and once a company pays the first time it must keep paying. Moreover, they may be against international law and could land a foreign company in trouble should there be any change in government or should there be any desire to clamp down on corrupt practices. Companies must very carefully weigh their options, and, if possible, sell their comparative advantage instead of trying to cut corners. Companies must maintain strict policies against graft but use their best judgment to determine what is acceptable and what is not.

Box 3

An Example of Misunderstanding Across Cultures

Consider the following scenario: Stacy, an eighteen-year-old American undergraduate traveled to an African country to visit the family of her African roommate. During her memorable stay with this family, Stacy witnessed first hand the legendary African hospitality as well as the warmth and caring that every member of the family extended to her. She was, indeed, spoiled by her host family. Also during her stay, Stacy became fond of one of the family's roosters. She eventually adopted the rooster as her pet and named him Brandy. Stacy would spend time feeding and petting Brandy so much that by the time her four-week stay in Africa was coming to an end, she had become very attached to the rooster.

On the eve of Stacy's departure from Africa, her host family held a meeting to decide how best to show, for the final time, their appreciation to Stacy for her visit. It was agreed that a sumptuous dinner be prepared in her honor. At dinner the hostess spoke up: "Stacy," she said, "we have noticed since your arrival at our house that you have taken a liking to a particular rooster. To show you our gratitude for your visit and to wish you well on your departure, we could see no better way than to serve you the rooster you have taken time to groom."

It is needless to state that Stacy went into shock. She was horrified, indeed, mortified at the thought of having Brandy for dinner. She quickly lost her appetite, excused herself, and made for the bathroom, to the total surprise and confusion of her host family.

In this situation, two things are apparent. The first is that Stacy's host family had the best of intentions in showing their utmost hospitality to please their guest. The only problem is that unlike in the United States where any animal can be a pet, in this particular ethnic group, only dogs and cats are considered to be pets. Nobody raises chickens as pets in this society. They are raised for food, and only those interested in eating them show the kind of attention that Stacy had shown to that particular rooster. The second thing is that Stacy was horrified at the thought of having Brandy, her pet rooster to whom she was so attached, for dinner. In America, pet owners often develop deep attachments to their pets and would never consider eating them.

Stacy's departure from her host family that had treated her so well and her pleasant and memorable experience in Africa became tainted by this problem caused by cultural differences which could have been avoided had she been aware of them.

DEALING WITH INDISCIPLINE AT THE BUSINESS AND SOCIETAL LEVELS

There is really no easy way for a business to deal with indiscipline at the societal level. One must bear in mind that every society is predisposed to lawlessness and indiscipline. The problem that most African countries face is not a lack of rules or regulations but the lack of enforcement of rules and regulations.

One must understand how things are done, which rules are respected, and which ones are not. In some countries people do not pay attention to traffic lights. It would be naïve, even dangerous, not to consider this fact when driving in the streets. One must ultimately develop a strong sense of adaptation based on common sense and information from US Embassy officials and reliable business associates.

ENHANCING WORK ETHIC AND IMPROVING WORKER PRODUCTIVITY

It is important to know that the productivity levels are likely to be lower than the levels found in the US because of low expectations and lack of skill. Africans are not lazy. They may be slow in accomplishing some basic tasks because, here again, there has not been any need to ensure more productive performance.

To obtain optimum performance from workers, one needs to motivate and lead them, as well as train them at the basic level. Obviously, the remuneration scheme must also reflect the emphasis placed on productivity and quality performance.

One must note that labor productivity varies world-wide. It depends on people's attitudes, skills, health and nutrition. People's attitude toward work and their preparation depend on their values and attitudes toward paid employment and their ability to be adventurous, as well as their views toward savings. These attitudes differ greatly in Africa, from ethnic groups that have been historically entrepreneurial to those that are less adventurous.

Also one must note that in Africa, the majority of the work force is employed in agriculture. The labor force is characterized by low wages, large wage differentials, rapid growth of labor supply, and underutilization of the existing labor supply. The labor market is characterized by segmentation or three-tiered employment structure: urban formal sector, urban informal sector, and rural sector.

The urban formal sector's employers are government, large-scale enterprises, bank, factories, etc. They pay the highest wages and employ the best workers. In the urban informal sector, the labor force operates outside the formal sector. Workers here are mainly hawkers, transporters, shopkeepers and those who work in curbside establishments. This sector provides jobs for migrants who couldn't be employed in the urban formal sector. It is, therefore, characterized by ease of access, lower wages than the formal sector. It is frequently suppressed by government in spite of the numerous services they provide. Finally, the rural sector consists mostly family labor. It is characterized not only by low wages but also by underemployment and underutilization of labor.

DEALING WITH
NEPOTISM

Collectivism is not a bad thing insofar as it is the basis for team-based production system, cooperation, and group dynamics. However, if a firm needs help with hiring staff, it must emphasize and ensure the need to search for the best, otherwise it may wind up with the relatives of the employer or it may find that ethnic origin may overtake merit in the hiring process.

The disadvantage of collectivism is that it prevents individuals from acting without group consensus. One observes that in organizations alliances (sub-groups) are formed within the larger group. Members of the alliances find themselves compelled to adopt the position taken by the sub-group. In this situation, it is difficult for individuals to act independently regardless of what their personal positions may be. Obviously this practice can lead to frustration in the process of negotiation, initiating change, or expansion. It may also be time-consuming and inefficient.

The majority of African societies are patrilineal, whereby family lineage is traced through the man's lineage. The African family is the unit of early development and socialization, the unit of production, and the unit of consumption. So, what affects the family, affects human development and socialization, production, and consumption patterns.

Attitudes and behavior are determined by family structure, extended family structure, village structure, and grouping by age, gender, and ethnic affiliation. One must, therefore, recognize the concepts of "family" and "extended family" which would give a clearer picture of the reality of the microeconomic powers, as well as the levels of social and economic decision-making. Family members are united by legal links and obligations of economic and religious nature, as well as by a precise body of rights and by human feelings and emotions. The extended family mostly does not correspond to a place or abode but to a series of solidarities among several people linked by blood or marriage.

THE THREE Ps OF AFRICAN BUSINESS:
PENSIVENESS, PATIENCE, AND PERSEVERANCE

The key to success lies in the 3 Ps: pensiveness, patience, and perseverance. **Pensiveness** demands that we think, use our heads and use common sense. Success also demands that we exercise a lot of **patience** because things are not going to happen so fast. Above all, we must **persevere** and be persistent, but polite.

IMPROVING INTERCULTURAL COMMUNICATION

Americans conducting business in Africa must be in a position to expect the difficulties involved in inter cultural communications because of the distinctiveness of cultural perceptions. By knowing what to expect one can minimize costly mistakes and compete more effectively with Europeans and Asians.

Larry Samovar and Richard Porter recommend that to communicate effectively in an intercultural setting, one must know oneself, consider the setting, seek to understand message systems, develop empathy, encourage feedback, develop communication flexibility, and avoid stereotypes. An individual will know himself by knowing his perceptions and how he acts on those perceptions. According to Samovar and Porter, the timing of discussion or communication—the appropriate time to talk about any particular subject—is vital. The authors also suggest that the social setting in which the communication will take place be seriously considered. By social setting, they mean such possible venues as office, bar, or café, or whether or not to sit on the floor. An understanding of the most appropriate social setting for a particular type of negotiation is very important for positive outcomes. Finally, Samovar and Porter recommend adaptation to social climate which denotes sensitivity to the mood and climate of the specific situation and adaptation to customs.

Samovar and Porter warn that foreigners must understand the meaning of gestures while avoiding the "no-no words," tribe and other derogatory terms. It is equally important to avoid a myopic view of people, stereotyped notions concerning gender, race, and culture, patronizing comments, an attitude of superiority, etc. Finally the authors state that the first step in developing empathy is "...to learn to accept that there are differences among individuals and cultures."[26] The authors also suggest the need to pay attention, be expressive, and avoid interpretation of the African cultural manifestations from the American culture's orientation.

Prolonged delays in response to even ordinary inquiries are not unusual. A friend living in the US wrote about six letters to a ministry in an African country before he got one response about his business inquiry. What he did not realize was that there were such major bureaucratic bottlenecks that even basic communication that requires a yes or no answer took months, and sometimes, years. It is, however, reassuring that many African countries have actually taken steps to clear this type of bureaucratic bottleneck.

Here is an example of the problems that can arise from communication between individuals of different cultures. While in Botswana, an American colleague decided to rent a car to conduct some business. When he realized that he was going to be late in returning the car, he called the car rental agency and told the agent that he had some delay and would be returning the car a little late. He was sure that he heard the agent say that there would not be any additional charge, or at least he came away from the discussion assuming that he understood the terms. The American arrived at the car rental office about one-half hour late and reminded the agent that he had called about his lateness. When he got his bill, he found, to his great surprise that he was actually billed for an extra day. He was confused and frustrated and could not understand what had happened.

As it turned out, the most probable explanation was that the agent could not tell the American outrightly on the telephone that he (the American) would be billed for an extra day in case of the late return of the automobile. In other words, the agent had difficulty saying no to the American. So the American learned a hard lesson in cultural differences and intercultural communication. Had he been better informed, he would have either anticipated the outcome in spite of the telephone discussion or read the nuances in the response given over the telephone. This means that he would have been better prepared to handle the situation.

In communicating, proverbs, analogies, prose, and metaphor are used and speech is often more implicit, but polite. Modesty is cherished and third party involvement, especially to communicate grievances is not uncommon. Negative feedback is preferably given and received in private, at the appropriate time. Open confrontations are avoided as much as possible.

Box 4

An Example of What Not To Do

Two individuals met at a cocktail party in the United States, one a young man from Ghana, the other, an elderly American man. As the dialogue ensued between the two individuals, the American whom we shall refer to as Joe asked Kofi, the Ghanaian: "Where you from?" "Ghana" responded Kofi. "Where's that," continued Joe." "Africa," responded Kofi. Do you Africans still live in trees? I mean are there like roads and houses in Africa?" asked Joe with great sarcasm. Infuriated, despondent, and insulted, Kofi hesitated for a moment, but determined not to loose his cool, responded: "Yes indeed, we do live in trees. We actually reserve the biggest tree for the American Ambassador in Accra." The evening became sour for the two individuals who, in the first place, came to the cocktail party to have fun.

What could bring about such an exchange? Ignorance? Prejudice? Whatever it is that brings about this kind of unpleasant exchange, that is what must be eliminated. For Africans do not live in trees. Indeed, Africans have never lived in trees, and the continent owes this preposterous and totally false portrayal to Edgar Rice Bourroughs, who never went to Africa and who through his utterly fictitious Tarzan series did more to damage the continent's image and perception than anyone else.

We must be very careful about how we compare other people to ourselves. "...Careful comparison of African and Western cultures shows that they share in common spheres of concern with the limits of the controls people can hold over their social and natural environment and with how they can reassert control or influence their worlds.."[27] It is important to recognize that the dominant American cultural patterns—equality, materialism, science and technology, progress and change, activity and work—do not necessarily differ from those of

Africans. The differences lie in the extent to which each of the patterns is demonstrated or believed in, and the way in which they are prioritized. Admittedly, a key difference between American and African cultures is that individualism dominates American culture while collectivism pervades the continent of Africa.

Encounters between cultures are never easy. One possible reaction to an unfamiliar culture is to consider the foreign culture to be "interesting," "strange," quaint," etc. and even "inferior," because it is different. A good example is the attitude that people often exhibit when reading cross-culturally. Writing about reading cross-culturally, Ann Carver states: "...the reader is filtering what she reads through the conceptual framework, assumptions, and values of her culture, and, as a result, is creating false "stories" that fit her own expectations." She warns that this reader gains no understanding of the culture. Carver uses three basic questions to capture the main essence of the problem of cross-cultural encounters: "Can Western readers accept the premise that people different from themselves can never be known, understood, or explained, and that it is all right? Can we identify the ways each of us deals with difference within our own cultures, the ways our cultures influence our dealing with difference, and the ways we see ourselves in relation to difference?"

These are pertinent questions that any Westerner visiting Africa or doing business in Africa must ask himself. Americans and other Westerners must strive to avoid what Ann Carver refers to as the "illusion of homogeneity," which, according to her, would mean that "If one can learn to see and accept the reality of others and their experiences, and stop there—without understanding or explaining them—one will have succeeded."[28]

5

UNDERSTANDING AFRICA

MYTHS AND FACTS

Anyone interested in doing business in Africa must understand that Africa—the ethnic mosaic—is not monolithic and that there is considerable ethnic and cultural diversity in the continent and within each country. It is equally important to understand the role that religion, especially Islam, has played and continues to play in shaping modern Africa. Understanding that these factors, together with the ethnic and interest group-based power structure, shape the conditions and relations that exist in each country helps a non-African to better grasp the national political and cultural dynamics.

Africa is the second largest continent, following Asia, and is three times the size of the United States. Africa consists of over 53 countries, the largest number of countries found in any continent. Africa is dynamic, having evolved and transformed over many centuries, during which time the forces of history, have given it a multifaceted identity, which still survives.

AFRICA IS A VERY DIVERSE CONTINENT

There is considerable ethnic and cultural diversity and complexity in the continent and within each country. In Africa, what country really means is a geopolitical entity arbitrarily 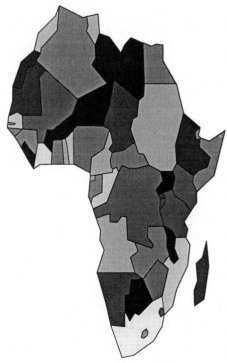 carved out by the colonial powers that has little bearing on existing ethnic realities. This partitioning of the continent took place during the 1885 Berlin conference that marked the partitioning of the continent and set the stage for the scramble for Africa. In the majority of cases, therefore, each African country is an artificial creation of Europeans. This means that the geographical delineation of each country has little bearing on existing historical and idiosyncratic realities of Africa's ethnic groups and nations.

Figure 2. The Diversity of Africa

Differentiating among Africa's social groups is a difficult undertaking. There are over 2,000 named African societal groupings in all and more than 1,000 African languages that differ from each other as much as English differs from French. Africa's political systems are diverse, ranging from democratic to non-democratic systems. Botswana, Senegal, South Africa, Ghana, etc. are examples of democracies.

There is equally great economic diversity in the continent, whereby rich and poor countries coexist. Using World Bank figures, a comparison of per capita income in 1994 shows Seychelles with $6,680; Botswana with $2,800; and Rwanda with $80.[29]

Also the physical environment shows climatic and vegetational diversity, consisting of temperate (Mediterranean), desert, savanna, humid tropical, and highland zones. In terms of land area, there are big and small countries. Sudan has a land area of 2,505,000 km^2, while Seychelles has only 45,000 km^2 of land area.

Colonial experience and the cultural legacy of colonialism also differ among African countries depending on the colonial power. Hence African countries can be categorized as anglophone (English-speaking), francophone (French-speaking), lusophone, (Portuguese-speaking), and hispanophone (Spanish-speaking). In terms of numbers, francophone and anglophone African countries dominate.

Most of contemporary Africa has been influenced by three basic cultures: the indigenous civilization, the Islamic culture, and the Christian/Western traditions. This is a triple heritage. Before the arrival of Islam, however, there was already an older triple heritage: An interplay of African culture, Semitic culture, and Greco-Roman culture. Ethiopia is an example of the ancient triple legacy where Christianity has flourished since the 4th century with Judaism and Greco-Roman social traditions. Nigeria is a good example of 20th century triple heritage.

Most historians agree to the fact that Africa had, before the arrival of Islam, great kings and great empires as well as elaborate technological skills before colonization. Also, there were traditions that were non-technical. So, on the one hand, there were the pyramids of ancient Egypt, the Ancient Zimbabwe, as well as the great empires of Ghana, Mali, Songhay, Malawi, Bornu, etc.

It is noteworthy that the controversy and constant antagonisms between indigenous and imported cultures is at the origin of conflicts between tradition and modernity, between city and countryside, between religious groups, between ethnic groups, and between the elite and the masses. This is the contradictory foundation on which contemporary African culture is based. Given the existence of thousands of highly diverse indigenous African ethnic groups, in reality, the term "African" is almost all they share.

ANGLOPHONE, FRANCOPHONE, AND LUSOPHONE AFRICAN CULTURES DIFFER

African countries can be categorized on the basis of their colonial experience, since all but a handful were colonized by Britain, France, Portugal, Germany, Holland, or Spain. The predominant colonial powers were Britain, France, and Portugal. It is, therefore, important to understand the fundamental differences between anglophone (former British or English-speaking colonies), francophone (former French colonies), and lusophone (former Portuguese colonies) Africa. Notably, these countries tend to maintain the legacy of their colonial experience in terms of trade, relations with each other, and world view. It is not uncommon to see a francophone African country totally indifferent or even unfriendly to its anglophone neighbor and vice versa.

The British colonial administration applied a system of "indirect rule," whereby they ruled their former colonies indirectly through local African leaders. They differed sharply from the more centralized assimilationist approach—in which the Africans were to be assimilated into European culture—adopted by the French and Portuguese. The result was that anglophone countries obtained independence with a greater proportion of their culture intact than the francophone and lusophone African countries. Because of these assimilationist imperatives adopted by the French and the Portuguese, Africans from francophone and lusophone African countries tend to be more Europeanized than their anglophone counterparts in terms of values, world views and even such things as mode of dressing and food habits.

Notwithstanding this stark contrast, a third dimension must be recognized. Because of the strong influence of Islam—which is not just a religion but also a way of life—the effect of assimilation on Africans is less in Islamic francophone countries (or in Islamic populations of francophone African countries) than in non-Islamic francophone African countries.

In general, all African countries suffer from the conflict of culture introduced by their experience with multiple cultural heritage, especially that resulting from the colonial experience. Colonialism created the cultural complex, identity crisis, and social dilemma in which Africans find themselves today. These problems have four basic dimensions. The first is the creation of the elite (by colonialism)—the urban elite—whose tastes, values, and way of life differ from those of the masses. The second is the problem, or rather conflict, of national identity and foreign domination which virtually all African countries currently face. The third is the conflict between people's (national) culture—literature, music, dance, theater, and art and foreign culture often embraced by a few privileged nationals. The fourth is the contradiction between the urban and rural, the modern and the traditional.

So at the same time that national pride drives people to try to find roots in the traditions in form of ethnic customs and traditions, songs, poems, theater, and dance, they also confront a mostly urban, foreign imported culture. This forces a certain form of duality in the way of life of many Africans especially the urban educated elite who have not completely cut their rural and traditional roots. This cultural duality must be understood in order to fully appreciate the dynamics of African business culture.

RELIGION AND BUSINESS IN AFRICA

The issue of the relationship between religion and economic development can be stated in the form of two main questions as it concerns Africa:

1) Is religion as it is lived and practiced in favor of, antagonistic to, or indifferent to productive effort?

2) Is the social ethic strong enough to prevent or exercise a sort of stranglehold on any form of change, or does it permit the questioning of some social values?

In Africa there are four major religions: Indigenous Traditional Religions, Islam, Catholicism, Other Christian Faiths.

Traditional Religions: Almost all African traditional religions perceive the world as magical, which does not necessarily constitute an irrational attitude, since if one believes in the magic of the world, the world becomes effectively magical. But this attitude is incompatible with research effort and individual responsibility. Traditional religion emphasizes collectivism as opposed to individualism thereby limiting the extent to which individualism plays a role in spurring adventurism, discovery, and entrepreneurship. It also limits the role of self-interest in engendering advancement. Like some other religions, it does not encourage the unknown to become known since it is deeply rooted in mysticism.

Catholicism: Because the Catholic church has long condemned purely financial activities which are considered forms of usury up to the 19th century, the origins of Capitalism were concentrated in Protestant and Jewish areas (enclaves). Growing up as a boy, the author remembers the priest proclaiming the virtues of poverty and the apocalyptic destiny of the wealthy. The influence of Catholicism in contemporary developing societies is today very profound because the separation between the spiritual and the temporal is more clearly defined in Christianity than in Islam. In addition, the Catholic Church preaches the sermon of "increase and multiply," which is no longer consistent with the long-term interest of individual households in African countries. Likewise, its vigorously condemning contraception helps in perpetuating the burden of extended family dependence that African workers and businesspersons bear since birth rates among Catholics will continue to be high.

Islam: Islam's attitude towards business and development has been an object of repeated debates and discussions. Islam in Western thought has often been associated with underdevelopment. In fact, from the 16th century, the Islamic world underwent a transformation which led to its domination by the Western world in the 19th century. The reason which is often given to explain the underdevelopment of the Islamic world is the "fatalistic" character of the religion. The fatalism does not signify avoidance of action but teaches that God does not reveal to anyone his destiny: thus "the belief in God does not prevent believers from getting medical care even though God has already fixed the date of everyone's death." It is, therefore, difficult to believe that the Islamic fate should constitute an obstacle to productive effort and innovation from this perspective. The problem however, is that certain practices associated with Islam in many African countries are antagonistic to business development. The first is polygyny and the second is the impact of Islam on economic activities. Even though polygyny can be rationalized in certain circumstances, it is totally in conflict with economic progress.

Although Islam supports industrial progress, it stipulates that this should be devoted to the production of commodities necessary for the harmonious and progressive raising of the standard of living of the people, since the "Production of luxuries is inconsistent with and repugnant to the spirit of Islam."[30] It is not easy to distinguish between what is a luxury good and what is not in a diverse and dynamic society. Islam also believes in the Divine ownership of resources, it is against the accumulation of wealth, and it prohibits interest and supports the Mudaraba (the Islamic interest-free banking system).

The Islamic belief in Divine ownership of material wealth negates the rights of humans to the ownership of their material possessions either as individuals or as a nation. Similarly, the Koran severely condemns accumulation of wealth: "Woe to him who pileth up wealth and layeth it by, thinking that his wealth would make him last for ever! He will be sure to be thrown into that which breaks to pieces."[31] Although Islam demands the highest truthfulness and honesty in trade and commerce and makes all dishonest earning in trade unlawful, we have seen that as in Christianity, the practice is sometimes far from the preaching. Furthermore, the hostility of some of the Imams and conservative Muslims toward secular education and the emancipation of women constitutes serious problems for development. The practice of *Purdha* which severely confines women, limiting their ability to effectively contribute to economic growth is a case in point. Much of the seeming paradox illustrates the fact that there seems to be a contrast between the ideology which would, in most cases, be progressive and the practice which is a different matter all together.

Other Christian Faiths: Since Protestantism is pro-business, it is not necessary to discuss it in full. However, such Christian sects as Jehovah's Witnesses found widely all over Africa, have certain extremist views about the role of the individual in the society that can create problems for business and economic development.

CONCLUSION

In the presence of increased and unprecedented Westernization, African societies and culture, always dynamic, are undergoing transformations including children leaving home at an early age and moving to the cities, the loosening of traditionally-defined gender roles, and the diminishing of age-based authority.

Africa's considerable cultural diversity, if understood, is not an impediment to successful American business. To manage these cultural differences, one must understand the need for personal relations and the role that connections play in African business and the African respect for hierarchy, titles, and age. One must also comprehend the concept of "African Time" and recognize it in making plans, as well as ensure that there is considerable follow-up. One must further understand the role that honor plays in business relations because this is important for mutual understanding and effective communication.

The American entrepreneur needs to realize that certain practices that are not tolerated or permitted in the US may be rampant in Africa and must draw the line, making a decision from the start and sticking to it. He or she needs to know how the rules operate and that because of lack of enforcement, often laws are openly broken. Further, the entrepreneur must understand that although African workers have a positive work ethic, they may lack the motivation and the skills for high productivity and that Africans tend to be communal, emphasizing collectivism instead of individualism. Likewise the American businessman or woman must note that there is often a clear definition of gender-based roles. The tendency to take decisions more slowly, looking for unanimity before acting, creates a reluctance to contradict or challenge the system. Finally he or she must have an abundance of patience and perseverance, and remember to follow up.

Intercultural business is always a challenge; African business is no different. But with the cultural knowledge presented here, the American businessman and woman, if they keep an open mind, should be able to proceed with confidence that they will reap the many profitable rewards the dynamic African market offers.

NOTES

[1]Shawna O'Grady has asked similar questions in her study of the Mexican business culture. From her findings, there are, not surprisingly though, many similarities between the Mexican cultural characteristics and the African cultural characteristics. This similarity is also true of African and Asian cultures. See Shawna O'Grady, "The Culture of Doing Business in Mexico," presented at Academy of International Business 1996 Annual Meeting, Banff, Alberta, Canada, September 26-29, 1996.

[2]US Department of Commerce, "Sub-Saharan Africa: The Last Frontier for U.S. Business Abroad," pp. 195-196, reprinted from the Fourth Annual Report to the US Congress of the *National Export Strategy*, October 1996.

[3]US Department of Commerce, 1996, p. 6.

[4]US Department of Commerce, 1996, p. 6.

[5]Keith Marsden and Thérèse Bélot "Private Enterprise in Africa: Creating a Better Environment." World Bank Discussion Paper No. 17, Washington D.C.: The World Bank, 1987, p. xiii.

[6]"A Comprehensive Trade and Development Policy for the Countries of Africa," A Report Submitted by the President of the United States to the Congress, Pulled from International Trade Administration Web Site, ND.

[7]Calvert New Africa Fund Web Page.

[8]Seymour Patterson, Verbal Communication, August 1996.

[9]US Department of Commerce, 1996, p. 6.

[10]"A Comprehensive Trade and Development Policy for the Countries of Africa."

[11]World Bank, *World Development Report 1996,* New York: Oxford University Press, 1996, pp. 189, 208.

[12]World Bank, International Financial Corporation, "Prospects for the Business Sector in Developing Countries," Discussion Paper No. 3, 1989, p. 26.

[13]World Bank, *World Development Report 1996,* pp. 192-193. Net private capital flows includes private debt flows—commercial bank lending, bond, and other private credits and nondebt private flows—foreign direct investment or portfolio investment.

[14]H. Ned Seelye (ed.), *Experiential Activities for Intercultural Learning,* vol. 1, Yarmouth, Maine: Intercultural Press, Inc., 1996, p. 10.

[15]Geert Hofstede, Cultures and Organizations: Software of the Mind, London: McGraw Hill Book Company, 1991, pp. 10-11.

[16]Alex Inkeles and Daniel Levinson, "National Character: The Study of Model Personality and Sociocultural Systems," in *The Handbook of Social Psychology,* 2nd edition, vol. 4, 1969, pp. 447ff.

[17]Geert Hofstede, 1991, p. 28.

[18]Geert Hofstede 1991, p. 36.

[19]Geert Hofstede, 1991, p. 51.

[20]Geert Hofstede, 1991, pp. 82-83.

[21]Geert Hofstede, 1991, p. 113.

[22]Keith Marsden, "African Entrepreneurs : Pioneers of Development." IFC Discussion Paper No. 9, Washington D.C.: The World Bank, 1990.

[23]Deborah Brautigam, "African Industrialization in Comparative Perspective: The Question of Scale," in *African Capitalists in African Development*, eds. Bruce Berman and Colin Leys, London: Lynne Reinner Publishers, 1994.

[24]Various authors have discussed issues relating to African indigenous entrepreneurship, notably Tom Forrest, *The Advance of African Capital;* D. B. Cruise O'Brien, *The Mourides of Senegal,* Oxford: Clarendon Press, 1971; Keith Marsden and Thérèse Bélot, ibid., Economics Department of the World Bank, "Prospects for the Business Sector in Developing Countries." Discussion paper No. 3, IFC, Washington D. C.: The World Bank, 1990, p. 18. Tyler Biggs, Gail R. Moody, Jan Hendrick van Leeuwen, and E. Diane White, "Africa Can Compete! Export Opportunities and Challenges for Garments and Home Products in the U. S. Market." World Bank Discussion Paper No. 242, African Technical Department Series, Washington D. C.: The World Bank. 1994.

[25]Larry A. Samovar and Richard E. Porter, *Communication Between Cultures,* 2nd edition, Washington: Wadsworth (Washington: Wadsworth), 1995, pp.275-300.

[26]Larry Samovar and Richard Porter, pp. 275-300.

[27]Larry Samovar and Richard Porter, ibid.

[28]Ann C. Carver, "Can One Read Cross-Culturally?" *Studies in Language Teaching, Linguistics, and Literature*, NO. 2, October 1996, pp. 161-167.

[29]World Bank, *World Development Report 1996*, New York:

Oxford University Press, 1996.

[30]A. Hashim, "Islam and Economic Problems," in *Some Economic Aspects of Islam*, Karachi, Umma Publishing House n.d., 34.

[31]A. Hashim, N.D., p. 31.

APPENDIX

AFRICAN CULTURAL CHARACTERISTICS

Titles, formality, and prestige are taken very seriously in African cultures

- People want to be properly greeted and properly addressed as Chief, Doctor, Engineer, Barrister, etc.
- People are expected to show a great deal of politeness and courtesy
- There are rigid hierarchies and centralized power in many organizations
- Employees work more for their boss than for the company

A lot of importance is placed on personal connections and relationships

- There is need for personal trust and need for establishing a trusting relationship
- A great importance is attached to family as well as the extended family
- Thus the notion of family may be more extensive than what we may see in the United States—there is often the use of brother or sister among people who are unrelated

African countries tend to be collectivist societies

- Getting into high positions is largely affected by family connection as opposed to education or merit

- Nepotism is a common feature in both public and private sectors.

Saving face is of utmost importance in the African culture

- People will go to great lengths to avoid losing face or bringing shame to themselves and to their family
- In trying not to disappoint Africans may say "yes" to avoid conflict since they are more oriented towards harmony than conflict

Time is not considered firm but flexible

- The African culture does not believe in making decisions quickly

HOW TO DEAL WITH PEOPLE IN AFRICA

- Try to pronounce peoples names as accurately as possible.

- Avoid patronizing people or clearly showing your prejudice, bias, or stereotypical beliefs.

- Avoid condescending behavior.

- Greet people or return greeting and inquire about their health and family before engaging in other inquiry, requesting service, or discussing business.

- Try to understand the hierarchy that exists within an organization and it is advisable to greet or address people by referring to their titles.

- Understand the meaning of gestures and know that a gesture that is acceptable in the United States may not be acceptable in some African countries.

- Avoid the use of offensive words and derogatory remarks.

- Learn to accept that there are differences among individuals and cultures.

- Avoid interpreting African cultural manifestations from the American or Western cultures orientation.

- Avoid myopic view of people, stereotyped notions concerning gender, race, and culture, patronizing comments, and attitudes of superiority, etc.

- Know that people different from you may never be fully known, understood, or explained, and that it is all right.

- Know that Africans are very religious people and that religion plays a major role in peoples way of life, attitudes, taboos and practices, and world view.

HELLRIEGEL AND SLOCUM'S LIST OF TYPES OF RESTRICTIONS, CONTROLS, AND THREATS THAT MAY BE ENCOUNTERED BY FOREIGN OPERATIONS OF US FIRMS

- Threat of nationalization

- Limitations on the expansion of foreign operations

- Limitations on the percent of ownership of foreign operation by US firms

- Nationality restrictions on who can serve as managers and directors of foreign subsidiaries

- Requirements to purchase needed materials and supplies from the host country, regardless of quality

- Restrictions on the amount of dividends from foreign operations that can be returned to the parent company

- Controls over the prices that can be charged

- Control on the amount of imports and exports

- Restrictions on flows of capital into and out of host countries

- Threat of war or political upheaval in within the country.

Collected from Don Hellriegel and John W. Slocum Jr., *Management,* Third edition, Philippines: Addison-Welsley, 1982, p. 144.

LIST OF AFRICAN COUNTRIES

Algeria, Angola, Benin, Burkina Faso, Botswana, Burundi, Cameroon, Cape Verde, the Central African Republic, Chad, Comoros, Congo, Côte d'Ivoire, Djibouti, Egypt, Equatorial Guinea, Ethiopia, Eritrea, Gabon, The Gambia, Ghana, Guinea, Guinea-Bissau, Kenya, Lesotho, Liberia, Libya, Madagascar, Malawi, Mali, Mauritania, Mauritius, Morocco, Mozambique, Namibia, Niger, Nigeria, Rwanda, São Tomé and Principe, Senegal, Seychelles, Sierra Leone, Somalia, South Africa, Sudan, Swaziland, Tanzania, Togo, Tunisia, Uganda, Zambia, Zaire, and Zimbabwe.

The United Nations in Africa

Among the United Nations (UN) agencies and programs, the UN Development Program (UNDP), Food and Agriculture Organization (FAO),World Health Organization (WHO), UN High Commissioner for Refugees, the UN Children's Educational Fund (UNICEF), the International Fund for Agricultural Development (IFAD), the UN Population Fund, United Nations Conference on Trade and Development (UNCTAD), the International Trade Center and the Protection of the Global Environment Fund are the most active in Sub-Saharan Africa.

WHERE TO GET MORE INFORMATION

PUBLICATIONS ON AFRICAN CULTURE

Paul Bohannan and Philip Curtin, *Africa & Africans* Fourth Edition, Illinois, Waveland, 1998.

Phyllis M. Martin and Patrick O'Meara eds., *Africa,* Second edition, Bloomington: Indiana University Press, 1986.

Mario Azevedo and Gwendolyn Prater eds., *Africa and Its People: An Interdisciplinary Survey of the Continent,* Kendall/Hunt, 1982.

PUBLICATIONS ON CULTURAL DIMENSIONS

Geert Hofstede, *Cultures and Organizations: Software of the Mind,* London: McGraw Hill Book Company, 1991, ISBN 0-07-707474-2

Larry A. Samovar and Richard E. Porter, *Communication Between Cultures,* 2nd edition, Washington: Wadsworth, 1995.

N. Adler, *International Dimensions of Organizational Behavior,* Second Edition, Boston, MA: Kent Publishing, 1991.

Geert Hofstede, *Culture's Consequences: International Differences in Work-Related Values,* Beverley Hills: Sage Publications, 1980.

PUBLICATIONS ON AFRICAN BUSINESS

"Sub-Saharan Africa: The Last Frontier for U.S. Business Abroad," (pp. 195-196) reprinted from the Fourth Annual Report to the US Congress of the National Export Strategy, October 1996.

Keith Marsden and Thérèse Bélot "Private Enterprise in Africa: Creating a Better Environment." World Bank Discussion Paper No. 17, Washington D.C.: The World Bank, 1987, p. xiii.

Tyler Biggs, Gail R. Moody, Jan Hendrick van Leeuwen, and E. Diane White, "Africa Can Compete! Export Opportunities and Challenges for Garments and Home Products in the U. S. Market." World Bank Discussion Paper No. 242, African Technical Department Series, Washington D. C.: The World Bank. 1994.

The African Business Handbook 1996-97 Volume 3. Published by 21st Century Africa, Inc. ISBN: 0-9638197-1-2, (pp. 480), $45

World Bank, International Financial Corporation, "Prospects for the Business Sector in Developing Countries," Discussion Paper No. 3, 1989, p. 26.

World Bank, World Development Report 1996, New York: Oxford University Press, 1996.

Business in Africa (formerly *SAFARA magazine*) published by Goldcity Ventures. London Address: Suite F11, Shakespeare Business Centre, 245A Coldharbour Lane, LONDON SW9 8RR, Phone: 0171-737 5933; Fax: o171-738-3613; E-mail: 100567,1243@CompuServe.com.

US GOVERNMENT PUBLICATIONS AND CONTACTS

Africa and the Near East Flashfax Hotline (202) 482-1064
Trade Information Center: 1-800-USA-TRAD
Office of Africa:(202) 482-5198
Office of the Near East:(202) 482-0878

National Trade Data Bank: The central repository for economic, commercial, marketing, and statistical information on foreign countries collected by 23 U.S. Government agencies. On the World Wide Web: **http://www.stat-usa.gov.**

"Sub-Saharan Africa: The Last Frontier for U.S. Business Abroad," (pp. 195-196) reprinted from the Fourth Annual Report to the US Congress of the *National Export Strategy*, October 1996.

United States Department of State, *Key Officers of Foreign Service Posts*, US Government Printing Office. Gives key information about US government officials, including commercial attachés in US missions abroad. To get a copy call: The U.S. Government Printing Office at (202) 512-1800 or fax (202) 512-2250

United States Department of State, *Diplomatic List*, US Government Printing Office. The U.S. Government Printing Office at (202) 512-1800 or fax (202) 512-2250. Gives a listing of Foreign missions and embassies in the United States as well as the diplomats, phone numbers and addresses.

The International Trade Administration publishes *Economic and Commercial Overview* of individual African countries. These are available by fax. To obtain a .FLASHFAX DIREC-TORY FOR SUB-SAHARAN AFRICA dial (202) 482-1064.

Business America, The Magazine of International Trade, published by the U.S. Department of Commerce, International Trade Administration, Washington D.C.

PUBLICATIONS FROM INTERNATIONAL ORGANIZATIONS

World Bank, *World Development Report 1996*, New York: Oxford University Press, 1996

World Bank, International Financial Corporation, "Prospects for the Business Sector in Developing Countries," Discussion Paper No. 3, 1989

Keith Marsden and Thérèse Bélot "Private Enterprise in Africa: Creating a Better Environment." World Bank Discussion Paper No. 17, Washington D.C.: The World Bank, 1987.

INTERNATIONAL BUSINESS

George F. Simons, Carmen Vásquez, and Philip R. Harris, *Transcultural Leadership: Empowering the Diverse Workforce,*

Houston, Gulf Publishing Company, 1993.

Vincent Guy and John Mattock, *The International Business Book: All the Tools, Tactics, and Tips You Need For Doing Business Across Cultures,* Lincolnwood, Illinois, NTC Publishing Group, 1996.

IMPORTANT WEB SITES

By far the most comprehensive web sites are:

- Africa Weblinks: An Annotated Resource List prepared by Ali B. Ali-Dinar UPENN: http://www.sas.upenn.edu/African_Studies/Home_Page/WWW_Links.html and

- Africa Business & Trade: http://www.sas.upenn.edu/African_Studies/About_African/www_trad.html

See also:

- Index on Africa at http://www.africanidex.africainfo.no/

- National Trade Data Bank: http://www.stat-usa.gov

- Virtual @frica at http://www.virtualafrica.com/tea/

- *African Profiles International Magazine*: http://www.productzoo.com/cgi-bin/tame/profiles/article.tam

- The World Bank Group: http://www.worldbank.org/

- Multilateral Investment Guarantee Agency

(MIGA): http://www.worldbank.org/ or http://www.worldbank.org/rmcvp/rmcguar.htm

- Panafrican News Agency: http://www.nando.net/ans/pana/FEED/P

- Nigeria.Com - Nigeria on the Net: http://www.nigeria.com/

- International Trade Administration - Trade Information: http://www.ita.doc.gov/

- Africa News on the World Wide Web: http://www.africanews.org/

- Africa Policy Home Page: http://www.igc.apc.org/apic/index.shtml

- United States Trade Representative home page: http://www.ustr.gov/

- Panafrican News Agency: http://www.nando.net/ans/pana/FEED/PANAFEED.html

- International Trade Administration-Trade Information: http://www.ita.doc.gov/

IMPORTANT CONTACTS

CONSULTING SERVICES

AFRIMAX, Inc. *International Business Consultants & Publishers*
P. O. Box 946 Kirksville MO 63501, U.S.A.
 Phone: (816) 665-0757; Fax: (816)665-8778
afrimax@msn.com

AMI Consultants
303 N. Central Avenue
Phoenix Arizona 85012
Phone: (602) 279-7278; Fax: (602) 279-7703

21st Century Africa, Inc.
818 18th Street, N.W., Suite 810
Washington, D.C. 20006
Phone: 202.659.6473; Fax: 202.659.6475

US GOVERNMENT DEPARTMENTS

Office of Africa
Room 2037
U.S. Department of Commerce
Washington D.C. 20230
Fax: (202) 482-5198

US Department of State 202-647-4000
African Public Affairs Office of the State Department
(202) 647-7371

The U.S. Government Printing Office
(202) 512-1800 or fax (202) 512-2250

United States Department of Commerce
International Trade Administration
Washington D.C. 20230

Foreign Commercial Service (FCS)
American Embassy Abidjan
Department of State
Washington, D.C. 20521-2010
Tel: (225) 21-09—79
Fax: (225) 22-24-37

Office of the U.S. Executive Director
African Development Bank
American Embassy Abidjan

Department of State
Washington D.C. 20521-2012
Tel: (225) 20-47-32
Fax: (225) 33-14-34

U.S. Department of Commerce
International Trade Administration
Trade Development, Advocacy Center
HCHB, Room 3814A
Washington D.C. 20230
Phone: (202) 482-3896; Fax: (202) 482-3508

INDEX

A

Abidjan, FCS and AfDB, 24
AfDB (African Development
  Bank), 24
affirmative action, for women,
  61
Africa
  and American foreign direct
    investment (FDI), 15
  countries of, 88
  cultural dimensions of, 37-54
  diversity of, 74-76
  equity markets, 20
  exports, 17
  Greco-Roman culture, 75
  import markets, 17
  information on, 89-92
  myths and facts about, 73-81
  publications on, 89-92
  questions to ask, 12
  social characteristics, 12, 54
African-African American
  Summit, 24
African-American Chamber of
  Commerce, 24

African culture
  characteristics, 86-87
  compared with American
    culture, 33 (table)
"African time," 12. See also
  time/timing
age
  managing cultural differ-
    ences, 58
  respect for, 12
  and status, 40-41
America. See United States
anglophone countries, 76-78
Angola
  emerging market, 20
  US trade in, 21
apprenticeship, and en-
  trepreneurial culture, 49
  (box)
Arab Africans, and negotiation, 59
art forms, and national pride,
  77-78
Asia
  and American FDI, 15
  investment returns, 16

PDI study, 39
attitude
   changes of, in Africa, 18
   vital to business success, 69
authority, and cultural dimensions, 34

B
Bélot, Thérèse, 18
Benin, social stability, 18
Berlin Conference (1885), 74
Bond, Michael, 35
Bornu, 76
Botswana
   democracy, 75
   intercultural communication, 70
   per capita income, 75
   trade and investment goals, 26
Brautigam, Deborah, 49 (box)
break times, 50, 61
bribery and corruption, surviving, 51
Britain. *See* Great Britain
Brown, Ron (commerce secretary), 22
bureaucracy
   business protocol, 59
   managing cultural differences, 69
Burkina Faso, social stability, 18
Burroughs, Edgar Rice, 71

(box)
Burundi, social stability, 18
business culture. *See also* entries under "cultural"
   and collectivism/communalism, 33 (table)
   and competition, 33 (table)
   and family, 42
   and fax usage, 42
   managing cultural differences, 55-72
   and modesty, 46
   and religion, 78-81
   and telephone usage, 42
business risks
   cautionary notes, 28
   safeguards, 25
business success
   3 Ps, 68-72
   rules for, 86-87

C
Calvert New Africa Fund, 19-20
Cameroon, social stability, 18
capital markets, 19-20
Carver, Ann, 72
Catholicism, and Capitalism, 78, 79
cautionary notes, 28
Central African Republic, social stability, 18
Chad, social stability, 18
Chevron Oil Co., 21

Christian/Western tradition, 75, 78
and Capitalism, 79
and gender roles, 46
and meeting schedules, 61
Clinton, Bill (President), report to Congress (1996), 22-24
Coca Cola Co., 21
"cocktail party" example, 71 (box)
collectivism/communalism, 12, 33 (table), 86
and business culture, 33 (table)
and cultural dimensions, 37
and nepotism, 67
and traditional religions, 79
vs. individualism, 42-44
colonialism
and African culture, 32
and cultural characteristics, 76-78
and Europeanization, 77
and foreign domination, 77
commodities, from Africa, 20
common currency, and economic development, 19
communication
criteria for success, 68-72
managing cultural differences, 56-58
tools for business success, 70
Comoros, trade and invest-ment goals, 26
conflict vs. harmony, 46-47, 77-78
Congo, social stability, 18
Constituency for Africa, 24
consulting services, 95
contract adjustments, 51
Corporate Council on Africa, 24
correspondence protocol, 59
corruption and bribery, 51, 63
Côte d'Ivoire
FCS and AfDb, 24
social stability, 18
US trade in, 21
courtesy, 40-41
Crane, Phillip (US congressman), 22
cross-cultural reading, 72
cultural characteristics, summary, 54, 58
cultural conflicts, 46-47, 77-78
and discipline, 12, 52, 65
cultural dimensions
African, 37-54
five, 34
4-D model, 35
indexes of, 39 (table)
LTO and STO, 35
Yorubas, 40
cultural patterns
American vs. African, 33 (table), 71-72
example of misunderstand-

ing, 64 (box)
currency devaluation, and economic reforms, 18

D
deadlines, flexibility, 62
decision making
and hierarchical structure, 41
managing cultural differences, 58
and time perception, 48
democracies, 75
despotism, no bar to trade, 27
discipline, 12, 52
managing cultural differences, 65
diversity
of Africa, 74 fig. 2, 74-76
and complexity, 32
economic, 75

E
East Africa
cultural dimensions index, 39 (table)
MAS, 45
economic development
Africa, 18-19
and common currency, 19
and religion, 78
economic diversity, 75
economic reforms, 18
ECOWAS (Economic Community of West African States), 19

education
and Islam, 81
profile, 26 (box)
Egypt, 76
elites
and colonialism, 77
and the law, 52
EMDB (Emerging Markets Data Base), 21
emerging markets, 19, 20 (table)
English-speaking countries, 76-78
entrepreneurial cultures
models of, 49 (box)
vs. traditional religion, 79
environment, 26 (box)
equity markets, in Africa, 20
Ethiopia
cultural dimensions index, 39 (table)
triple cultural heritage, 75
US trade in, 21
ethnicity. *See* diversity.
Europeanization, and colonialism, 77
European monopoly, 25-26
exports, from Africa, 17
Exxon, 21
eye contact, 53

F
face-saving, 47, 50-51, 86
and managing cultural differ-

ences, 61
failure, and honor, 51
family structures
  and business culture, 42
  and Catholicism, 79
  importance of, 67-68
  patrilineal, 67
fax
  and business culture, 42
  Dept. of Commerce no., 63
FCS (Foreign Commercial Service), 24
FDI (foreign direct investment) of US, 15
feedback, and cultural differences, 70
femininity. *See* women
follow-up, and cultural differences, 62
foreign domination, and colonialism, 77
formality, and managing cultural differences, 58
4-D cultural model, 35
France
  colonialism, 76
  PDI study, 39
  UAI, 47
French-speaking (francophone) countries, 76-78

G
Gabon
  social stability, 18

trade and investment goals, 26
Gambia, social stability, 18
GATT (General Agreement on Tariffs and Trade), 25
GDP (gross domestic product), Africa, 28
gender, social roles, 45-46
geopolitical boundaries, 74
gestures, vital to business success, 69
Ghana, 76
  cultural dimensions index, 39 (table)
  democracy, 75
  example of what not to do, 71 (box)
  eye contact in, 53
  social stability, 18
  trade and investment goals, 26
  US trade in, 21
gifts, 53
GNP (gross national product), Sub-Saharan Africa, 28
go-betweens, 59
graft, 51, 63, 82
gratuities, 51
Great Britain
  and American FDI, 15
  colonialism, 76
  PDI study, 39
  UAI, 47
Greco-Roman culture, 75

greetings
   importance of, 40-41, 53
   and managing cultural differ-
      ences, 58
   protocol of, 58
Guinea, 18
Guinea-Bissau, 18

H
handshaking, 53
harmony vs. conflict, 46-47, 77-
   78
health and nutrition, 26 (box)
hierarchy, 12, 86
   and decision making, 41
   importance of, 40-41
   managing cultural differ-
      ences, 58
hispanophone countries, 75
Hofstede, Geert, 34, 35, 38, 39
   (table), 43, 45, 47
holidays, 61, 62
honor
   and business relationships, 61
   personal, 12
   and tradition, 50-51
hospitality, and cultural differences, 64 (box)

I
IBM Corp., 21
   social/cultural study, 35, 39
IDV (individualism index), 39
   (table), 43
IFC (International Financial

Corporation), 20
Igbos. *See under* Nigeria.
ima mmadu, 44
IMF (International Monetary
   Fund), and African re-
   forms, 18
implementation, managing cultural differences, 56-58
import markets
   in Africa, 17
   comparison by countries, 17
income, per capita. *See* per
   capita income.
individual freedom, 26 (box)
individualism, 26 (box)
   and cultural dimensions, 34,
      35, 37, 38
   vs. collectivism, 42-44
   vs. traditional religions, 79
Inkeles, Alex, 34, 35
institutions, and power distance, 38
intercultural communication,
   57-58
intermediaries, 59
International Court, the
   Hague, 25
international publications, 91-
   92
investment
   Calvert New Africa Fund,
      19-20
   and long-term growth, 29
   returns

comparison by countries, 16
stabilizing influence, 27
USDFI, 28
Islam, 75-80
and assimilation, 77
avoid pork and alcohol, 60
break times, 50
and Capitalism, 79-80
and culture, 32
and gender roles, 46
importance of, in Africa, 73
and meeting schedules, 61
Mudaraba (banking system), 80
Ramadan, 62

J
Japan, and MAS, 45
Jehovah's Witnesses, 81
Judaism, and Capitalism, 75, 79

K
Kenya
cultural dimensions index, 39 (table)
Kikuyus, 52
social stability, 18
US trade in, 21
work ethic, 52
kickbacks, 51, 63, 82
"know thyself", 68-69
kporakpoism, 44

L
labor market, characteristics of, 66
languages, of Africa, 74
language usage, vital to business success, 69
Latin America, investment returns, 16
Latin countries, PDI study, 39
law, and elites, 52
leadership
managing cultural differences, 56-58
methods, and PDI study, 39
left hand, 53
letters, protocol for, 59
Levison, Daniel, 34, 35
LTO (Long Time Orientation), 35, 38
business considerations, 62
lunch breaks, 50
lusophone countries, characteristics of, 76-78

M
Madagascar, 18
Malawi, 18, 76
males. *See* masculinity
Mali, 18, 76
management
of cultural differences, 55-72, 56 fig. 1
importance of follow-up, 62
markets
and African reforms, 18
emerging, in Africa, 20

(table)
equity, 20
import, 17
size, 17
Marsden, Keith, 18, 49 (box)
masculinity
  and cultural dimensions, 34, 37
  and family lineage, 67
  in Muslim countries, 61
  social roles, 45-46
  vs. femininity, 45-46
MAS (masculinity index), 39 (table), 45
Mauritania, 18
MBO (management by objectives), 39
McDermott, James (US congressman), 22
meeting schedules, and cultural differences, 61
MIGA (Multilateral Investment Guarantee Agency), 25
modesty, and business culture, 46
motivation, factors influencing, 66
Mourides. *See under* Senegal.
Mozambique, , 18
Mudaraba (interest-free banking system), 80
Muslims. *See* Islam.
myths and facts about Africa, 73-81

N
national identity, and colonialism, 77
negotiation
  and Arab Africans, 59
  and collectivism, 67
  and hierarchical relationships, 41
  strategies and cultural differences, 59
nepotism, 44, 86
  managing cultural differences, 67
NGOs (non-governmental organizations), trade initiatives, 24-25
Niger, 18
Nigeria
  cultural dimensions index, 39 (table)
  emerging market, 20
  entrepreneurial culture, 49 (box)
  eye contact, 53
  formality, 58
  Igbos, 44, 49 (box)
  and nepotism, 44
  personal courtesy, 40-41
  social stability, 18
  trade and investment goals, 26
  triple cultural heritage, 75

US trade in, 21

O

OPIC (Overseas Private Investment Corporation), 24
organizations
  and personal courtesy, 41
  and power distance, 38

P

patience, and business success, 68
Patterson, Seymour, 21
pay, and motivation, 65, 66
PDI (power distance index)
  and cultural dimensions, 38, 39 (table)
pensiveness, and business success, 68
per capita income
  Africa, 17, 26 (box)
  Botswana, 75
  Chinese, 17
  comparison by countries, 17 (table)
  Rwanda, 75
  selected countries, 75
  Seychelles, 75
perseverance, and business success, 68
personal relationships/connections
  and business success, 12, 41-42, 86
  managing cultural differences, 60
personal sensitivities, 53
personal titles
  examples of, 41
  importance of, 12, 40-41
  managing cultural differences, 58
  use of, 86
political instability, no bar to trade, 27
political reforms, 18
political systems, 74-75
polygyny, and Capitalism, 80
Porter, Richard, 57, 68, 69
Portugal, colonialism, 76
Portuguese-speaking countries, characteristics of, 75-78
poverty, 26 (box)
prayer times, importance of, 61, 62
prestige, importance of, 40
productivity
  factors influencing, 66
  low, 12
  and religion, 78
  and work ethic, 52
profitability, of Africa, 15-16
progress profile, 26 (box)
Protestantism, and Capitalism, 78, 79, 81
P's of African Business, 68-72
publications on Africa, 89-92

R
Ramadan, 62
Rangel, Charles (US congress-
    man), 22
reforms, 18
regional blocs, 19
religion. *See also* Catholicism,
    Christian/Western, Islam,
    Judaism.
    and business in Africa, 78-81
    importance of, 73-74
    vs. research and responsibil-
        ity, 78-79
respect, and managing cultural
    differences, 58
"rooster" example, 64 (box)
rules for business success, 86-87
Rwanda
    per capita income, 75
    social stability, 18
S
SADC (Southern African De-
    velopment Community),
    18
Samovar, Larry, 57, 68, 69
self-conception, and cultural
    dimensions, 34
Semitic culture, 75
Senegal
    democracy, 75
    entrepreneurial culture, 49
        (box)
    eye contact, 53
    Mourides of Touba, 49 (box)
    social stability, 18
    Wolofs, 53
    work ethic, 52
Seychelles
    per capita income, 75
    size, 75
    trade and investment goals,
        26
Sierra Leone
    cultural dimensions index, 39
        (table)
    social stability, 18
social culture, 12, 54. *See also*
    diversity.
    appropriate settings, 69
    inequality, and cultural di-
        mensions, 37
    organization of, 33 (table),
        86-87
    stability of, 18
    status issues, 38-39
    values, and religion, 78
Songhay, 76
South Africa
    cultural dimensions index, 39
        (table)
    democracy, 75
    MAS, 45
    trade and investment goals,
        26
    US trade in, 21
Spain, PDI study, 39
Spanish-speaking countries, 75

status, and age, 40-41
stock markets, in Africa, 19
STO (Short Time Orienta-
    tion), 35, 38
strategic planning, and cultural
    differences, 55-72
success, rules for, 86-87
Sudan, size, 75
Sullivan, Leon, Rev., trade ini-
    tiatives, 24
Sweden, and MAS, 45

T
Tanzania
    cultural dimensions index, 39
        (table)
    social stability, 18
tariffs and trade, 1994 GATT,
    25
"Tarzan" example, 71
telephone, and business cul-
    ture, 42
Texaco, 21
3 Ps of African Business, 68-72
time/timing. *See also* LTO,
    STO
    adapting to African concept,
        61
    "African time," 12
    cultural perceptions of, 48,
        50
    and decision making, 48
    and managing cultural differ-
        ences, 59

and meeting schedules, 61
and personal relationships,
    60
vital to business success, 69
titles, personal, 12, 40-41, 58,
    86
Togo, social stability, 18
trade
    and investment goals, 26-27
    trade initiative bill (1996), 22-
        24
tradition
    and business relationships,
        12, 61
    and honor, 50-51
    vs. modernity, 76
    religion vs. research and re-
        sponsibility, 78-79
training, for managing cultural
    differences, 57

U
UAI (uncertainty avoidance
    index), 39 (table), 47
Uganda, social stability, 18
uncertainty
    avoidance of, 34, 35, 39
        (table)
    harmony vs. conflict, 46-47,
        77-78
United Kingdom. *See also*
    Great Britain.
    and American FDI, 15
United Nations in Africa, 88

United States
  benefits of African trade, 26-27
  businesses in Africa, 15-29
  cultural characteristics, 54
  cultural comparison with Africa, 33 (table)
  cultural dimensions index, 39 (table)
  Department of Commerce, 16, 22, 63
  FDI (foreign direct investment) distribution, 15
  MAS, 45
  PDI study, 39
  trade in Zimbabwe, 21
  trade with Sub-Sub-Saharan Africa, 25-26
  UAI, 47
United States government
  departments of, 95
  President's report to Congress, 19, 22-24
  publications and contacts, 90-91
  support for African trade, 22
  support for American firms, 22
  trade initiative bill, 22-24
US-Africa trade, 29-30
USAID (United States Aid for International Development), 24
USDIA (United States direct investment in Africa), 28
USFDI (United States foreign direct investment), 28

W
Web sites, 93-94
West Africa
  cultural dimensions index, 39 (table)
  MAS, 45
Westernization, and gender roles, 46
Wolofs. *See under* Senegal
women
  and affirmative action, 61
  and cultural dimensions, 34-35, 37
  and handshaking, 53
  and Islam, 81
  social roles, 45-46
  vs. masculinity, 45-46
work ethic
  positive in Africa, 12, 52
  and worker productivity, 65
World Bank, and African reforms, 8
WTO (World Trade Organization), and US trade initiative bill, 23-25

Y
Yoruba
  nepotism, 44
  personal courtesy, 40

Z
Zambia
  cultural dimensions index, 39
    (table)
  social stability, 18
Zimbabwe, 76
  social stability, 18
  trade and investment goals,
    26
  US trade in, 21

Order Form

🖨 Fax orders: (816) 6658778

📠 Telephone orders: Call Toll Free: 1(888) 41AFRIMAX. Have your
   AMEX, Optima, Discover, VISA or MasterCard ready.

💻 On-line Orders: AFRIMAX@MSN.COM

🖃 Postal Orders: AFRIMAX Inc. P.O. Box 946
   Kirksville, MO 63501, USA
   Tel: (816) 665 0757

Please send the following books:

I understand that I may return any books for a full refund—for any reason, no
questions asked.

_____

_____

_____

❏ Please send the *African Business Newsletter* to me FREE.

Company name:_____

Name:_____

Address:_____

City:_____State:_____Zip_____ - _____

Telephone: (_____)_____

Sales Tax:
Please add 7.75% for books shipped to California addresses

Shipping:
Book rate: $2.00 for the first book and 75 cents for each additional book
(Surface shipping may take 2 to 4 weeks). Express shipment will require addi-
tional cost.

Payment:

❏ Check

❏ Credit card: ❏ VISA, ❏ MasterCard, ❏ Optima, ❏ AMEX, ❏ Discover

Card number:_____

Name on card:_____Exp. date:_____/_____

Call toll free and order now

Order Form

🖷   Fax orders: (816) 6658778

☎   Telephone orders: Call Toll Free: 1(888) 41AFRIMAX. Have your
      AMEX, Optima, Discover, VISA or MasterCard ready.

💻   On-line Orders: AFRIMAX@MSN.COM

✉   Postal Orders: AFRIMAX Inc. P.O. Box 946
      Kirksville, MO 63501, USA
      Tel: (816) 665 0757

Please send the following books:

I understand that I may return any books for a full refund—for any reason, no
questions asked.

_____

_____

_____

❏ Please send the *African Business Newsletter* to me FREE.

Company name:_____

Name:_____

Address:_____

City:_____State:_____Zip_____ - ____

Telephone: (_____)_____

Sales Tax:

Please add 7.75% for books shipped to California addresses

Shipping:

Book rate: $2.00 for the first book and 75 cents for each additional book
(Surface shipping may take 2 to 4 weeks). Express shipment will require additional cost.

Payment:

❏ Check

❏ Credit card: ❏ VISA, ❏ MasterCard, ❏ Optima, ❏ AMEX, ❏ Discover

Card number:_____

Name on card:_____Exp. date:_____ / _____

Call toll free and order now

Order Form

📠 Fax orders: (816) 6658778

☎ Telephone orders: Call Toll Free: 1(888) 41AFRIMAX. Have your
   AMEX, Optima, Discover, VISA or MasterCard ready.

💻 On-line Orders: AFRIMAX@MSN.COM

🖃 Postal Orders: AFRIMAX Inc. P.O. Box 946
   Kirksville, MO 63501, USA
   Tel: (816) 665 0757

Please send the following books:

I understand that I may return any books for a full refund—for any reason, no
questions asked.

_____

_____

_____

❑ Please send the *African Business Newsletter* to me FREE.

Company name:_____

Name:_____

Address:_____

City:_____State:_____Zip_____ - _____

Telephone: (_____)_____

Sales Tax:
Please add 7.75% for books shipped to California addresses

Shipping:
Book rate: $2.00 for the first book and 75 cents for each additional book
(Surface shipping may take 2 to 4 weeks). Express shipment will require addi-
tional cost.

Payment:

❑ Check

❑ Credit card: ❑ VISA, ❑ MasterCard, ❑ Optima, ❑ AMEX, ❑ Discover

Card number:_____

Name on card:_____Exp. date:_____/ _____

Call toll free and order now